Everyone's Guide to

ONLINE DATING

Some other titles from How To Books

Meet Your Match
How to find and keep the man or woman who's right for you

The Carer's Handbook
Essential information and support for all those in a caring role

Meat and Two Veggies
How to combine meat and vegetarian meals without having to cook separate dishes

How to Grow Your Own Food
A week-by-week guide to wildlife-friendly fruit and veg gardening

Getting Out of Debt and Staying Out
Face up to financial denial and free yourself from money worries

howtobooks

Please send for a free copy of the latest catalogue:

How To Books
Spring Hill House, Spring Hill Road,
Begbroke, Oxford OX5 1RX, United Kingdom
info@howtobooks.co.uk
www.howtobooks.co.uk

Everyone's Guide to
ONLINE
DATING

How to find love and friendship
on the internet

SHIMRIT ELISAR

howtobooks

Published by How to Books Ltd,
Spring Hill House, Spring Hill Road,
Begbroke, Oxford OX5 1RX, United Kingdom
Tel: (01865) 375794. Fax: (01865) 379162
email: info@howtobooks.co.uk
www.howtobooks.co.uk

British Library Cataloguing in Publication Data
A catalogue record for this book is available from the British
Library

ISBN 978 1 84528 186 1

Cover design by Baseline Arts Ltd, Oxford
Cover illustration by David Mostyn
Illustrations by Zephyr Pfotenhaur
Produced for How to Books by Deer Park Productions, Tavistock
Typeset by Pantek Arts Ltd, Maidstone, Kent
Printed and bound by Cromwell Press Ltd, Trowbridge, Wiltshire

Contents

About the Author

Shimrit Elisar is an online dating expert with 15 years' experience of dating and socialising on the Internet. She spent over five years working as an online moderator monitoring and advising customers on some of the largest message boards, online forums and dating sites in the UK. Although she is not a nerd, Shimrit was one of the first people to use the Internet for social purposes, as well as being one of the first women on the world's first chat room. She has lived in three different countries, worked as a journalist in two different languages and has travelled extensively around the world. She currently works for Allegran Limited, one of the UK's leading online dating companies.

Acknowledgements

I am greatly indebted to the following people, whose help and support helped make this book happen:

- Ryley and Tony, who did more for me than I could possibly mention in a single line or even a page (so I'm not even going to try)

- (Dr.) Deep, who started the whole thing off by giving me a job in spite of everything I said to him

- Ruthie Elisar (my mom), who shared her professional opinion with me and so helped me realise I was on the right track

- James and Laura, who were there from the very beginning (and beyond) and gave me lots of practical ideas whenever I needed some

- Marisa, whose input and feedback helped me put things in perspective and whose encouragement often came in handy

- Gavin, who donated his time, his critiquing skills and his willingness to wait in the wings to be called (and also his understanding when he wasn't)

- Bill, who kindly provided me with research materials and didn't complain when I forgot to give them back

- Camilla, Peter, Diz, Bob and everyone else who occasionally forced me to get out of the house

- Ergin and the CRM all-stars, Godfrey, Raied and the dev boys (and girls), Jake, Adrian and all the others at Allegran who made my working (and writing) life better

Last but not least, I wish to thank all my various case studies, friends, family members, research subjects and well-wishers who shared their stories, experiences and tips with me.

Thank you all!

Preface

If we could go back in time to the last days of the 20th century, pick a random UK town and ask the first person we saw what they thought about online dating, we would be lucky to get more than a blank stare or a raised eyebrow. 'Meet people on the Internet? That's crazy! Why would anyone want to do that?'

Nowadays, practically everyone is doing it.

Most of us know at least one person who's tried it, if not many more. In fact, stories about online dating are in the papers almost every day, as well as on TV and on the radio. What we have here is a craze, a phenomenon – a whole new method of dating that has completely changed the lives of many people.

I probably don't need to tell you all this. If you weren't already considering online dating, you wouldn't have picked up this book in the first place. Maybe you're even dating online already, but want to learn more about the subject so you can get better results.

Online dating can be an amazingly useful tool. Like any other tool you need to learn what it can do for you and how, before you can use it effectively. You need to learn its limitations so you can work around them and you need to get the feel of it so that you can find your own method of making it work for you. The purpose of this book is to help you understand the inner workings of online dating so you can get what you want out of it, whatever that might be.

This book grew out of my personal experience of dating online as well as my professional experience of working in the online dating industry. It's based on many hundreds of case studies that I've come across during 15 years of both working and socialising on the Internet. As part of my work, I've met many wonderful, intelligent people who were unintentionally hurting their own chances of finding love online. Most of the mistakes they made would have been easy to avoid with a bit of forward planning and an understanding of how online dating works. I wrote this book in order to address such problems and offer easy, straightforward solutions.

Because online dating is still a relatively new concept to most people, it still suffers from hype, scaremongering and the prevalence of much unnecessary jargon. I tried to avoid all of these in this book and aimed, instead, to give an unbiased, clear picture of the subject.

I wholeheartedly believe that there is someone out there for everyone. Maybe online dating will be your means of finding that someone, maybe not. You'll never know until you've given it a go. The time to start is now.

I wish you good luck in your search and hope that this book will help you find what you are looking for.

Shimrit

A note about genders

In order to simplify things, I have chosen to use the masculine gender for pronouns and collective nouns throughout this book. This, to me, seems less annoying than using 'he/she' or 'his/her' when writing about stuff that could apply to both sexes. I realise that this may occasionally paint an askew picture and for this I apologise. It was a matter of simple convenience, nothing more.

Dedicated to my grandparents,
who fell in love against all odds
and stayed together for the
rest of their lives.

Chapter 1

An introduction to online dating

In this chapter you will learn:

- What online dating is all about

- Things you need to know before you start

- What makes online dating different

- Naming your objectives

What is online dating?

Online dating, as you probably know, is simply the name given to the process of meeting and socialising with people on the Internet. The term 'online dating' itself is rather inaccurate: people generally don't 'date' on the Internet – they just use it to make initial contact. A more accurate term would have been 'online introductions', but that doesn't sound nearly as catchy.

Online dating is now a highly popular activity: approximately ten million people in the UK use online dating sites every month. In the USA, where Internet dating is now virtually a mainstream activity, the number is even higher.

Although most people associate online dating with dedicated dating sites, there are other means of using the Net to socialise. These will be discussed in Chapter 12 of this book and include platforms such as social networking sites, message boards and chat rooms. If you take all these into account, you will realise that billions, rather than mere millions of people are using the Internet for social purposes every day.

What's in it for me?

People turn to online dating for different reasons; what you get out of it largely depends on what you want to achieve. It's a highly versatile medium that is aimed at fulfilling a variety of needs.

Using the Internet you could:

- Expand your social circle
- Find activity partners
- Find new sexual partners
- Fall in love
- Find your next husband or wife

Some people are comfortable with the prospect of communicating with people in writing over the Internet and some prefer more traditional methods like phone calls or meeting up in person. If the thought of spending your spare time chatting online doesn't appeal to you, don't worry. Using online dating does not necessarily mean spending long periods of time exchanging messages or emails. Many people nowadays choose to keep their online interaction time to a minimum and there are sites where this form of online dating is actively encouraged. On the other hand, if you want to take your time and be more cautious that's perfectly acceptable too.

A brief history of online dating

Most people think about the World Wide Web when they think about online dating. The truth is, online dating predates the invention of the Web itself and goes back to the early days of the Internet. Back in those days, when the Internet was a plain, text-only medium, people used to make new friends by means of simple chat software, multi-user games and discussion groups. Surprisingly, early Internet users still managed to fall in love with each other, even though their less nerdy friends all thought they were crazy. With the invention of the Web, operating systems like Microsoft Windows and user-friendly chat programs such as ICQ and MSN Messenger, even less technically minded people started using the Internet to communicate with others.

Sadly, as the Internet became more popular, it also became more open to abuse. Chat rooms, previously thought of as the best means of online social interaction, became infested with spammers and perverts who ruined the experience for everyone. It was only a matter of time until dating websites started appearing, in order to provide a safer, more convenient alternative. Dating sites have now become one of the most popular ways of meeting people online. As a result, they have evolved into a multi-million pound industry, which is still growing every day.

Will online dating work for me?

Simply put, anyone can try online dating. However, your level of success will depend on several different factors.

Using the Internet, you can connect with thousands of new people without ever having to leave the house. This makes online dating particularly useful for those who fall under the below categories:

- People who are generally unable to go out and socialise regularly such as single parents, busy professionals, and those who are bedridden or disabled
- People with small social circles that lack suitable singles (recent divorcées, people in rural areas and anyone who's recently moved to a new city)
- People who want to know more about their potential dates before meeting them in person
- People who do not enjoy the loud social situations that are usually involved in the traditional dating process and are seeking an alternative

While dating sites are a great way to help you meet people, they cannot transform anyone's personality overnight or perform miracles. Those who fall under the below categories are not likely to benefit from their online dating experience:

- People with severe psychological or behavioural problems
- People who are still recovering from a bad break-up and are not yet ready to start dating again
- People who expect fast results with zero effort on their part

Online dating requirements

The technical stuff

Dating sites are designed to be as simple as possible to use, but there are still a few things you will need before you can embark on your search.

The most important requirement is a basic understanding of how to send and receive emails and how to use a web browser. Dating sites will generally assume you know how to do these things; some even have disclaimers saying they won't be able to help you if you don't. Knowing how to scan and upload pictures onto a website will also be useful, as photos are a key feature of online dating. Some dating sites offer support for people who are unable to digitise photos but you can't always count on it.

If you want to make use of some of the fancier features that are available on some dating sites (such as video and voice chat) you will need to familiarise yourself with the workings of web cameras and microphones. Although not essential, these are usually quite simple to use and can certainly make your experience more enjoyable.

Helpful attitudes

Not everything about online dating is down to technical knowledge. Being in the right frame of mind is also important. First and foremost, you need to have faith. If you convince yourself that you're never going to find love, you'll end up with a self-fulfilling prophecy. Millions of people all over the world find love online every day. If you want to join them, the first step is making yourself believe that it's possible (or at least not impossible).

While such optimism (or suspended disbelief) will work in your favour, it's also essential to have reasonable expectations. Putting it bluntly: there are no quick fixes. Cases where people go online and find their prince or princess charming within minutes/hours/days are as rare as people bumping into their soulmate on the bus. Yes, it does sometimes happen, but if you expect it to, you may be greatly disappointed.

During my time as a moderator, I came across a large number of people who joined a dating site and expected to be immediately united with their ideal man or woman. Unfortunately for those people, online dating is not the lottery; it's more of an investment. If you want to give it a real try, you will have to put time, effort and thought into the experience. Be willing to spend time (and often money) looking for the right site and the right people, be willing to go on a lot of dates and, most importantly, be willing to go back to the drawing board until you find what (and who) you want.

Common myths and misconceptions

When talking to people about online dating I have realised that there is still a huge amount of misinformation out there. While the stigma associated with it is dying out, people still bring up the same concerns again and again. If the below statements ring true to you, you may be surprised when you find out what things are really like.

Online dating is only for geeks

This may have been true back in the early days when only computing students and hardcore computer nerds knew what the Internet was. Nowadays, when people from all walks of life use the Internet every day, things are rather different. How many people you know use email either as part of their work or socially? How many of them used it 10 or 15 years ago? Times have changed, the Internet has changed and the world has moved on. Online dating is designed to be simple even if you don't know that much about computers. As a result, the people who use this method now are a pretty varied bunch.

Online dating is full of freaks

I won't lie to you: there are freaks out there. When you start dating online you will come across them sooner or later. The Internet has always been the preferred mode of communication for people who found it difficult to handle standard social situations. There was once a famous cartoon published in *The New Yorker* that showed dogs sat in front of a PC. The caption read: 'On the Internet, nobody knows you're a dog'. This, to me, sums the whole thing up beautifully: even the most unappealing, socially inept individuals can shine online and pretend they are well adjusted and attractive.

Being able to communicate with people without showing your face or stepping out of the house has an obvious appeal to such people. Luckily, now that the world has discovered the other advantages of dating on the Internet, social ineptness is not the only reason people choose to do it. In fact, many intelligent, professional and even trendy people turn to online dating because it's so simple and effective. The weirdos that you've heard of are still there, but they are merely a small portion of the online population, which is now a more accurate representation of the world we live in. You needn't let them put you off.

Online dating is unsafe and full of liars and scammers

This is still a major concern among those who are new to online dating and the Internet in general. Many people seem to still deem the Net unsafe. Certain members of my family, for example, still refuse to use their credit cards online for fear of having their details stolen. Those same people would quite happily hand over their card to a waiter at a restaurant, without fully considering the possible dangers of putting their trust in a complete stranger. People have been committing card fraud for years – long before the days of the Internet. Have they stopped using the old methods, now the Internet exists? Of course not, it's just that the Internet is new and we have a tendency to mistrust anything we don't fully understand.

The same goes for online dating. Of course some people out there lie and cheat, but adultery and fraud are not recent inventions. There are no more liars online than there are offline. After all, the people on the Internet exist in the real world too; they are not some kind of alien beings. Using the same common sense you'd use to sniff out those people in real life (plus the handy information available later on in this book) you can easily avoid these fraudsters and enjoy a safe and healthy dating experience.

Online dating is better (or worse) than traditional dating

Some people will tell you that online dating is far superior to traditional dating, while others will say it's grossly deficient. Frankly, neither of these is true. Online dating is just another way of meeting people. It has advantages and disadvantages like anything else and is not guaranteed to work for everyone. The only way to tell if it will work for you is to give it a go and see what happens.

Online dating will solve all your problems

It's amazing how many people turn to online dating expecting a miracle cure for everything that's wrong with their lives. Sadly, reality is not quite as straightforward as that. The act of looking for love online rather than offline is not in itself enough to guarantee good, long-lasting relationships. If you had a bad dating pattern, for example, where you found yourself repeatedly attracted to unsuitable people, this pattern would likely follow you until you stopped to deal with its causes. The medium of online dating alone would not be enough to stop it from repeating itself. This isn't to say that you should stop all human contact until you're sure you are 'perfect' (because none of us ever are) but be aware that it takes more than signing up to a dating site to fix any damaging relationship patterns or to heal a broken heart.

Online dating is a method used only by young people

For every person who thinks online dating is the realm of the geeky and the freaky, there is one who believes he is too old and 'uncool' to start searching for love online. While it's true that younger people are generally more comfortable with using the Net (as well as mobile phones, gadgets etc.) there are plenty of older people who use computers every day. The fact of the matter is that if you can send an email and use a web browser, you have all the skills you need to use an online dating site – regardless of your age.

You don't need to learn how to program and you won't be expected to use 'textspeak' to communicate with others (though some people choose to, for reasons I may never understand). The best news is, though, that whatever age you are, you will be able to find people of the same age group online.

The Internet is a place where you can get away with being rude and offensive for fun

For many people, the online dating experience is quite novel: and why not? It's different, it's entertaining and can even be quite silly and surreal at times. Sadly, sometimes it's too easy to forget that there are real people on the other side of the line; people with real feelings that can be hurt. Those users may be reduced to nothing more than a picture and a bit of text on our screens, but that doesn't mean they deserve to be treated in a disrespectful manner.

Insulting someone's looks or making racist and otherwise bigoted comments are things that are not tolerated online in much the same way they are frowned upon anywhere else. People who act in this way, generally find themselves kicked off their dating sites very quickly – and for a very good reason.

Dating online means you are desperate

This is a natural progression from the days when people who published lonely-hearts personals in the paper were seen as desperate. Luckily, this dated stigma is finally dying out.

If instead of saying you were unhappy with your love life, you said you were unhappy with your job, no one would criticise you for scanning the wanted ads for a better one. This may seem pretty obvious to you and me, yet it was only during the second half of the last century that people moved away from the notion that one's job was for life. Up until then, you would have met with scorn if you'd consciously tried to have a change of career at any point in your life.

For some reason, even though we now allow ourselves to actively attempt to improve the professional part of our lives, we may still be reluctant to do so when love and relationships are concerned. There is absolutely nothing wrong with admitting to yourself that you want to share your life with someone. There is also nothing wrong with wanting to put yourself out there in order to improve your chances of meeting that someone. Luckily, more and more people now realise this and are willing to take control of their love lives. Social attitudes don't change by themselves: they change as we realise that the world we live in is not the same one our parents lived in. Millions of people are dating online every day and the world is changing with them. Join them and you too can be a part of a revolution, if not a global one, then at least a personal one.

Online vs traditional dating

When I say that online dating is revolutionary, I really mean it. In many ways, the dating process is completely reversed when meeting someone on the Net. It's good to have an understanding of how things work before you jump in, so you can be aware of what makes online dating different.

The advantages of online dating include:

Earlier deal breakers

In traditional dating, we rely on our five senses, as well as our intuition, our emotions and our intellect in order to gauge our attraction to someone. Often, our intellect is engaged last, after we've already decided we are physically attracted to that person.

One of the main problems with traditional dating (as us online dating professionals love to point out) is that being physically attracted to someone or even being in love with him is no guarantee of your compatibility. Here is an example of a scenario that is, unfortunately, all too common.

> A woman I know in her late thirties, has recently ended a ten-year relationship with a man after finding out that, unlike her, he never wanted to have children. Although he had never lied about it, she had always assumed he would change his mind. When he didn't, she had no choice but to leave him. Needless to say, they were both devastated.

Such fundamental disagreements, known in the industry as *deal breakers*, are incredibly common and include other things such as smoking/drinking habits, political orientation, religion, ethnicity, etc. These are the fundamental differences that make it impossible for two people to form a successful relationship. Cue the main advantage of online dating and the reason why it's so successful among thirty-some-things with a long history of dating behind them.

In the world of online dating, the deal breakers are among the first things you will see when you browse people's profiles. From the first time you look at someone's profile, you will be able to tell whether he smokes, whether or not he wants kids and many other useful things, all depending on the dating site you are using. Imagine trying to ask a person you've just met whether or not he wants to have children: he would be out of the door before you could finish the sentence!

On the Internet, such behaviour is more than acceptable: it's practically built in to your registration process when you join a dating site. By specifying such information in your profile, you can instantly filter out unsuitable matches.

While knowing that person X wants to have babies does not in itself guarantee you would find him or her attractive or interesting, it does tell you that if you did, you would be able to develop your relationship to the desirable extent without coming across nasty surprises in the future.

Anonymity and control

For those who are reluctant to let strangers into their lives straight away, online dating affords an easy way of being in control of the dating process without giving away too much personal information too soon. Of course, chatting to someone online and finding him OK may not always be a guarantee of his ultimate sanity, but being able to maintain a level of privacy while communicating with someone can only be a good thing. On dating sites, the person on the other side won't even know your real name or email address unless you choose to share these with him. The best thing is, you will still be able to communicate quite happily until you decide whether you want to take things further.

Keeping your options open

One of the things that made online shopping so popular is the fact that it takes far less time to window-shop online than it does to travel from one shop to another and compare prices. Online dating is similar in the sense that it's much easier to browse user profiles and chat to different people than it does to go on the same number of dates. This means that you can have quite a busy social life, without ever leaving your desk.

You can still keep your options open even when it comes to meeting up in person. Most reasonable people won't expect you to have decided whether or not you are attracted to them based on a few online conversations. As a result, it's perfectly acceptable for both men and women to meet up with a selection of different people before making their mind up. However, it's also perfectly acceptable to cancel planned dates if you feel that you've already found the right person.

Now we come to some of the possible disadvantages of online dating.

False intimacy

One of the stranger issues that you may encounter is the issue of false intimacy. Online interaction only provides you with some of the information required in order to form a complete opinion of a person. The rest is filled out by your brain, based on your hopes, desires and fears. If you are new to online dating, you may find it hard to believe you could fall in love with someone based only on a picture, some personal blurb and a few text-based conversations. You may be shocked to discover that, in reality, you don't even need a picture. I'm always amazed anew at how much you can learn about what a person is like by simply exchanging emails. It's very possible to be won over by someone's personality without ever having seen his face. While such feelings usually grow over time, rather than appear instantly, it's very common to quickly develop a certain affinity with someone online or build up expectations based on someone's profile.

The difficult thing is remembering that the person you are talking to may really be quite different from the image you have constructed in your mind.

Social vs antisocial dating

When we think of traditional dating we usually think of clubs, pubs and other loud places where people congregate. I am not here to tell you that those methods are dated and ineffective in the face of online dating. On the contrary, I think they work pretty well for some people, with the added benefit of getting those people out of the house and into the company of others. While this form of social dating can be fun, it has obvious flaws. If it didn't, online dating would never have been invented.

Not everyone in the world is a loud, extroverted social butterfly who can walk up to a complete stranger on the dance floor and introduce himself. Social dating can therefore lend itself to much shallowness, putting some people at an obvious disadvantage.

Online dating offers those with a shyer disposition the chance to compose themselves and approach people in a more gentle manner, thus levelling the playing field. However, chatting on the Internet can become highly addictive and can end up keeping you from going out and interacting with people in a less detached manner. Spending too much time at home on your own in front of the PC can be quite damaging when done exclusively. It's important to try and find a balance between the two dating methods. Your goal should always be to meet up in person as soon as you feel comfortable.

The personal checklist

Often, people come to online dating with only a vague idea of what they want to achieve. This, I believe, is why so many people find that they spend much time online without getting very far. Being vague about what you want is fine if you just want to have a look around and check out the different possibilities, but if you want to get anything more out of the experience, you'll be better off thinking in advance about your goals. This is true even if you are only interested in flirting or casual dating, but is especially important if you are serious about finding love. It's worth spending the time it takes to work out what you really want to find, before setting off on your search.

The following list of questions is meant to get you thinking about where you are now and where you want to be. Think of this exercise as preparation for a journey, like marking your position and ultimate destination on a map before planning a route. Be as honest as possible; this is for you and you alone. The clearer you are about your goals, the easier it will be for you to achieve them. Don't be tempted to abandon your real goal (such as finding a wife or a husband) even if you think it may not be possible to achieve. Choose the goal you would want to achieve in an ideal world where everything is possible.

Write down your answers somewhere so you can refer to them if and when you need to.

Your goals

- What made you want to try online dating?
- What are you hoping to get out of the experience?
  - Friendship/socialising
  - Casual dating/sex
  - Serious dating/love
  - Marriage
  - I want to find out what all the fuss is about

The person you would like to meet

We all have our vision of a perfect partner. While in reality we may sometimes compromise, in an ideal world we wouldn't have to. Write down the things that make up your ideal partner. Be as detailed and descriptive as possible and try to go beyond physical attributes.

- What qualities must he have (looks, character, profession, aspirations, religion, ethnicity, hobbies, level of income, etc.)?
- What qualities must he *not* have (the 'deal breakers' or turn-offs)?

Where are you now?

Like everything else in the world, online dating is a venture that is likely to be more successful if you set off on the right foot. These questions should help you assess your own starting position so you can see where you are in your life.

- How do you feel about your love life at the moment?
- Not taking that into account, how do you feel about the rest of your life?
- List six things you like about yourself

■ List three things you dislike about your life or about yourself that you would like to improve

■ How do you feel about your chances of finding love?

If you have answered these truthfully, you should now be closer to understanding your position. Were any of these questions difficult to answer? Most of us find it easy to think about things that make us complain but more difficult to think of what makes us happy. Ideally, though, you should be able to think up answers to all of the above questions.

Sadly, some people turn to online dating (and dating in general) in an attempt to compensate for other parts of their lives that are lacking. Unfortunately, relationships that form out of this kind of need are not likely to be good and long-lasting. To put things bluntly, this means that if you are generally unhappy with all aspects of your life, you may not be in the best position to try online dating at this time. This isn't to say that you can't or shouldn't try it or even that you wouldn't get results. All it does is highlight the need for you to look at other areas of your life and bring yourself to a level where you are happy with yourself before bringing somebody else into the equation. Similarly, if you are pessimistic about your chances of finding love, you could end up with limited success unless you consider the reasons behind this pessimism and address them. If you wholeheartedly believe you're incapable of finding someone, you will most likely prove yourself right. If you tried online dating at this point, you would take any temporary setback as a sign that you were right and stop trying. You must get yourself to a point where you are at least open to the possibility of finding love and happiness, if you are to ever succeed.

Chapter 2

Finding the right site

In this chapter you will find out about:

■ The different types of dating sites

■ Finding and choosing a site

■ How to assess sites and avoid scams

■ Dating site reviews

The different types of dating sites

I recently spoke to a woman who was researching the subject of online dating for a TV documentary. 'The first thing I realised was that there are just so many dating sites out there,' she told me. 'I spent hours looking at different sites and getting nowhere. Every site I looked at claimed to be the biggest and the best; I didn't even know where to start! God only knows what I'd have done if I were actually looking for a date…'.

Most people who try online dating end up overwhelmed when looking at the various sites. The online dating boom has meant that there are now literally thousands of dating sites out there competing for your attention and money. I like to think of them as the virtual equivalent of pubs or clubs: places where people congregate and socialise. Just like pubs, some sites will be to your liking and some won't. The problem is that it's often impossible to tell whether or not you will like a site without trying it out. This can get quite exhausting and time-consuming if done on a regular basis.

So where do you start? It helps to have an understanding of the different types of sites you can choose from. At first glance, no two dating sites look exactly alike, because the web designers who build them want them to appear unique. When we look closely, though, all dating sites fall under one or more of several simple categories.

Paid sites vs free sites

Some sites will want to charge you for their services, whereas others won't. Unfortunately, it's usually hard to distinguish between the two types, as most let you register for free. Usually sites won't talk to you about money until you have signed up, uploaded a picture and located some people you would like to speak to. When you try to message your potential dates, an annoying message will appear and ask you to pay up. Until that point, it's often impossible or very difficult to find any information about pricing on the site.

Paid sites
Prices for paid sites differ greatly from each other and there is no real industry standard. Expect to pay about £20 a month for full membership to an average UK site but foreign sites may vary. Longer membership periods generally cost less per month than the standard monthly membership.

Paid dating sites operate as subscription sites, much in the same way magazines and book clubs do. The industry standard is 'uninterrupted membership', which means that once you put your credit card details in, you will keep getting charged until you contact the company in writing (an email is usually fine) and tell them to stop charging you. This is usually stated in the terms and conditions, although not always in an obvious place.

Most paid sites will offer a free trial, but some will ask for your credit card details at this stage. If they do, it means they are likely to start charging you at the end of the trial, unless you actively cancel your membership. Make sure you read the terms and know when those charges are likely to be taken.

Most sites will not refund you for partial use of their services. If you sign up for a month and change your mind after a week, you would still be charged for the whole month. This is another reason why it's worth noting in advance the exact date and time when charges will be taken from your account and set a reminder to cancel a few days in advance.

Some people have asked me how I can justify working for an online dating company that charges money for its services, when love is something all people deserve to have for free. I agree entirely: love should be free and so should food and shelter and warm clothes in winter. Unfortunately, until food and housing are free, the people who build and maintain dating sites need to make a living like anyone else. Remember that dating sites don't sell love; they sell the opportunity to meet others in a (hopefully) fun and secure way. Think of a dating site as a virtual club where your entry fee pays for the bouncer who keeps the troublemakers out and for the furniture you sit on while you chat.

But enough of my standing on soapboxes, the truth is there are free sites out there you can use if you don't want to pay for your dating experience.

Free sites

At this point, you may be wondering why anyone would want to pay for dating services at all, when the exact same features are offered for free elsewhere. But, as the saying goes, there is no such thing as a free lunch.

Dating sites are not that easy to run. They are extremely high-maintenance operations that require large amounts of powerful computers in order to function, as well as dedicated teams of employees to keep the sites safe, handle any technical issues that may arise and answer customers' queries. All this costs money, sometimes a lot of money. Free sites usually get this money from advertising, which often means their main priority is keeping their advertisers happy. Sadly, this can mean the site will be full of obtrusive adverts, pop-ups, pop-unders etc. To make matters worse, your personal details and email address would often be sold on to third parties who use them to send unwanted 'offers' and 'newsletters' (otherwise known as spam or junk emails). You may even be required to download applications onto your computer that include 'spyware' or 'adware' – bits of software that sit on your hard drive and report your web-browsing habits to companies that send you nasty pop-ups based on that data. Not all of the free sites are that dodgy, of course, but many are. This is another case where it pays to read the terms and conditions, as well as the privacy policy of each site you want to join.

Because free sites are so easy to join and require no financial commitment, they often attract more than their fair share of scammers who see them as an easy way of meeting their next victims without parting with any money themselves. Most free sites are not very well moderated and so the responsibility of filtering out the good from the bad lies mostly on the end user: you.

Such sites are also popular hang-outs for the less serious daters such as those looking for a quick shag or those having a look around out of sheer curiousity. Paid sites are generally better moderated and offer better customer service, as they rely on the membership fee to exist. The money issue also tends to deter the low-end users such as scammers, perverts etc. from joining. As a general rule, the more expensive a site is to join, the more likely it is to cater to serious daters who are looking for long-term relationships.

If you are undecided about dating online, you may be tempted to join a free site as a risk-free method of assessing what's out there. However, depending on the site you choose, this may not be your best option. You may be better off signing up for a free trial on one of the paid sites, as explained in greater detail below.

Although many of the free sites out there are annoying to use, there are some that are actually very good. Many people have found love on free dating sites, with the added benefit of not having paid for the pleasure. I have listed a few good free (and cheap) sites at the end of this chapter and the list is in no way complete.

General membership sites, orientation sites and niche sites

Any dating site you come across will come under one of the following categories.

General membership sites

As their name would suggest, general membership sites are those with broad membership. They are not geared towards a particular group but are open to anyone looking to try online dating. The big, well-known branded sites fall under this category, as well as many smaller sites aspiring to the same market position. On general sites you will find a large selection of online daters with a variety of interests, age groups, ethnicities etc. Good general sites will offer detailed search criteria in order to help you narrow down your search.

Orientation sites

There are sites out there that cater to large parts of the population, united by a single attribute such as race, ethnicity, sexual orientation or religious belief. These sites are sometimes referred to as lifestyle sites, though personally I prefer the term orientation sites. Shaadi.com, for example, is an orientation site catering to Asian daters, while gaydar.co.uk is an orientation site aimed at the gay and lesbian community. Orientation sites are often large (if successful) and entertain a variety of daters, much like general membership sites. The only difference is that all daters are likely to be of one general orientation.

Niche sites

Niche sites cater to groups united by more specific factors. A niche site can be a site aimed at people from a particular location, those who share a particular hobby or an alternative lifestyle and those who belong to a particular scene. Examples include sites for bikers, Goths, pet owners, media professionals, etc. These sites, by definition, usually have a smaller membership base.

Advantages and disadvantages of general membership, orientation and niche sites

When coming to choose between the different types of sites, you should first think about your lifestyle and hobbies and assess the extent to which you would like your partner to share these lifestyle choices. Any site with around a million or so members, is likely to have a good cross section of the population dating on it. Unless you have an extremely unusual lifestyle, chances are you will be able to find people who match your preferences on any large, well-established dating site. However, you will also find many people who don't. While general sites commonly let you specify things like religion and ethnicity and display them on your profile, they don't always allow you to search and filter results according to those characteristics. If your particular niche involves an interest, a hobby or a scene, you will probably have to list these on your profile in the description or interests section and hope for the best. Most general membership sites don't let you run searches based on interests.

The main advantage of general membership sites is the numbers. This is particularly true if you are from a small town or village. A search performed on a large membership site will likely return matches in your area, whereas a smaller niche site may not.

Orientation sites also have a large membership base and are a happy medium if you want to meet people with whom you have one particular aspect in common.

Niche sites are only really useful if you belong to a particular subculture or enjoy a lifestyle that goes beyond the mainstream. By joining a particular niche site you guarantee that the people you meet will share your lifestyle choices and/or interests. However, as such sites are usually small, you may still struggle to find people you find attractive and interesting, especially if you are from a small town and want to meet people in your area.

At the moment, most specialised niche sites are still American-based (apart from those aimed at people from particular locations elsewhere) and so may not have a large UK membership base. This, however, is changing as the online dating market is growing all the time.

Niche sites are often close-knit communities, where many people place a lot of importance on the particular aspect of their lives the site caters for. While some people join such sites in order to find someone who shares some of their hobbies, others join because that particular hobby is their whole life. If you only have a casual interest in the subject of the site you joined, you may find you have little in common with many of the other people there.

Branded sites

There is a growing trend of dating sites attached to or branded by newspapers, magazines, TV channels, etc. These are often not autonomous, but a pretty 'front' for one of the big general membership sites. In such a case, joining a branded site is no guarantee that the people you meet there will share your interests, political leanings or orientation. Sites that are not run by the company that owns the brand will usually say who they are powered by somewhere on the dating page. You can check the bottom of the page or the search form for clues.

Domestic vs international sites

Using a foreign site
The online dating craze originated in America, which would explain why so many dating sites are based in the USA. The American market still offers the widest choice of sites. Most of the big free sites are American-based, as well as a wide array of specialised niche sites, orientation sites etc.

Some of the bigger American sites now have dedicated UK branches. Others have large numbers of UK members on offer. Using a site like that should be much the same as dating on a British site. All sites let you specify location for potential matches, so you would only be shown local people if that is what you want.

If you are looking for a particular niche site, you will still most likely end up using an American site, simply because there are more choices available. You may well find a substantial UK membership on some of those, though others may be less forthcoming.

Because the pound is often quite strong against the dollar, the exchange rate will often work in your favour. Using a foreign pay site can therefore save you quite a bit of money, although some sites have now started charging UK members in pounds and have adjusted their pricing accordingly.

Using domestic sites

British sites are, by definition, geared towards the local population and will often include features designed specifically for UK daters. Mobile dating, for example, is now a common feature in the UK, but practically unheard of elsewhere. Mobile dating allows you to get notified by an SMS message whenever someone contacts you on the site. Sometimes you can even send and receive messages from people on the site via your phone.

Another advantage of domestic sites is the fact that many UK sites let you pay for their services by cheque, which, apart from being handy if you don't have a credit card, is a good way to avoid those sneaky recurring charges.

When things go wrong

These advantages aside, the main differences between domestic and international sites become apparent if anything goes sour with your experience.

Companies based in the UK have to conform to local laws so you would likely have better recourse if anything went wrong.

Domestic sites will also have the advantage of local support teams that operate during UK business hours. The moderating and customer service teams would be able to easily cooperate with the police if anything goes wrong such as in cases of scams or antisocial behaviour on the site. If your support team sits in another country, getting in touch with them could be difficult or annoying. When you do, you may find that the laws they follow are not the same as those followed by domestic companies.

Telling the difference

It's not always easy to tell whether a site you are using is in the UK or not, until the payment stage. The currency the prices are quoted in is usually a good indication.

Another way of telling where a site is based is by reading the site's privacy policy or terms and conditions, which should have a clause specifying which country's laws they conform to. If a site does not have a privacy policy available anywhere, ask to see one before you sign up. If one does not exist, the site could well be dodgy.

A note about 'adult' or sex sites

Although they fall under the niche or general orientation categories, sex sites deserve a special mention. They are usually referred to as adult sites, although obviously, all dating sites are already aimed only at adults.

People who join these adult sites do it because they want to get laid. That is all you really need to know. If you happen across a site like that, you will recognise it straight away, because it will be full of pictures of naked men and women. Members of such adult sites can search by sexual preference, fetishes, etc. as well as the usual age/sex/location model. These sites usually cater for both single members and those who are already in a relationship, such as swingers, etc. Most of the rules and practices described in this book, with the exception of the safety tips, do not apply on sex sites, where just about anything goes. Unless you are only interested in sex, you will find nothing of use on such sites.

Choosing a site

You can now start narrowing down your search by rereading your answers to the questions at the end of Chapter 1.

You may wish to search for a site based on your specified goals, such as a site for people who want to get married or one for people who just want to flirt. Now look over the list of qualities you would like in your partner. Could any of these be a theme for a niche or orientation site? Someone who wrote down 'must love cycling' on his list, for example, may benefit from dating on a cycle-enthusiasts' niche site. If you are a Christian, you could look for an orientation site offering dating services for Christian singles.

Search engines

Here's a quick tip about using search engines. People who are new to search engines usually only type one word or phrase in when searching for something ('dating', for example) and end up bombarded with thousands of results. Typing a longer string of words is usually preferable to the more basic search, as it narrows the results quite significantly. Searching for the word 'plumber', for example, would bring up too many results. You would be better off adding words like 'London' or 'CORGI' if you were looking for a CORGI-registered plumber in London. You may be tempted to think then, that searching for 'overweight biker dating Scotland', for example, would be better than simply inputting 'biker dating'. In my experience, though, using too many words to search for a dating site is not a good idea. Stick with the most important aspect of the kind of people you want to find and add only that word to your search: 'muslim dating', 'overweight dating', 'disabled dating' are all good examples. Once on the site, you can refine your search further and add physical characteristics etc.

Is this the right site for me?

Even if you have narrowed down your search to a particular type of website and know what you're looking for, you will still have quite a few sites to choose from. As a rule, I would say that you should visit and have a quick look at five dating different sites at least before you sign up for any free trials. This should give you a basic understanding of what's out there. When assessing a site, look at the following details to decide whether you should sign up to its services:

■ Does the site load quickly or is it slow? Are there any error messages or broken links?

■ Look and feel: does the site seem simple to use? Can you find your way around it easily?

■ What features does the site offer? All sites should allow you to upload a profile and a photo. Some sites will also allow you to upload voice clips and video. Does the site offer a real-time chat function as well as messaging? Are there any other useful features such as *icebreakers* (see Chapter 6)?

Now run the free search concentrating on the following:

■ Are there enough people fitting the criteria you specified? We are looking for quantity here and not quality as of yet. There should be at least one full page of people who match your search criteria, otherwise it may mean the site is lacking in suitable matches for you.

■ How many of these people would you consider as potential matches? Obviously, the more the merrier, but don't be put off if most of your finds are not immediately attractive to you. If you run a basic search and find one or two people you think may be interesting, then that's a good sign, even if you didn't get a large list of matches. At this stage, though, it's more important to see if the *type* of people who frequent the site appeals to you in principle. For a good indication of what you have to look forward to, scan through the profiles and concentrate on the text parts: the general information about the users and the stuff they write about themselves. After reading a page or so of such profiles, you will know whether the site has the sort of vibe that's right for you. Think of it as checking out a bar or a club to see if it has the right clientele before actually looking for a date there. Do you like the way these people express themselves? Do any of them sound like they would be fun to spend any time with? Do you share any interests? When checking out pictures, try not to concentrate too hard on whether or not you are attracted to each person and concentrate instead on their style and the general feeling you get. Could any of these be possible friend-material, even if you didn't find them immediately appealing?

■ If you run a basic search on a site that also offers matching features (such as personality tests etc.) the results may be deceiving. A quick search could show you a random selection of members with plenty of unsuitable people. A search based on more personalised matching criteria could reveal people you may actually like. Most sites that offer such features will let you try out their matching system for free. It's worth giving it a go and running a more informed search before giving up on such a site.

■ You can often tell a lot about a site and its members from the sign up process. Dating sites try to cater for their clientele and so will include questions that have an appeal to the type of people they expect will visit the site. Those sites that have been around for a while and are successful will have probably evolved by adding things based on user feedback. Their sign up process can therefore be quite revealing. For example, a general membership site that asks you to specify whether or not you are a vegetarian may have enough vegetarian daters to make this an issue. Obviously, the absence of such a question does not necessarily mean a site is devoid of vegetarian members, but if it's there, you can safely assume it's there for a reason.

The free trial – making the most of it

Choose the best two or three sites out of the ones you visited and register for the free account so that you can run a more detailed search. You should not be asked for your credit card details at this point. You might want to create a new email address with one of the free email services (Hotmail, Gmail etc.) for the occasion, as some sites will tend to email you frequently (and the free sites may sell your email address on). If the search results are to your liking, you will want to consider signing up for a free trial. This is where you will be asked for your card details so that the company can start billing you for membership at the end of the trial. Not all sites offer a free trial, but it is quite common. If the site you are on doesn't offer one, you can try the cheapest/shortest membership option instead.

Tips and Tricks

Free trials are usually very short – a few days at the most – so you should make sure that you get enough out of them. Here are a few tips and tricks.

- Only sign up for one free trial at a time. Even if you want to join a few sites, don't spread yourself too thin. Give each trial your full attention. Once you have finished with one, you can go on to the next one.

- Read the terms and conditions. I know I am repeating myself, but this is really, really important. By signing up to a free trial you are entering a binding contract. Always know exactly what it is you're (electronically) signing.

- Have the text for your profile and your photo(s) ready before you sign up for the trial. Don't waste precious time by composing the perfect profile during the trial; do it when the clock is not ticking.

- Search, search again and contact everyone you think could be worth talking to: this is what you're here for.

- Don't be tempted to use the free trial as a means of luring people away from the site in order to save you money. You may think it's clever but really it would only make you look cheap. It's also unsafe, because you would be sacrificing your anonymity.

- If you don't like the site, remember to cancel your membership before the free trial expires. Make sure you know when that is and how to cancel.

Avoiding scammers

Sadly, not all dating sites out there exist to help you. Some exist to scam people out of money. Luckily, they are few and far between and are generally easy to avoid. Here are a few warning signals that should make you suspect something is not quite right.

Sites that make you pay before running a search

This is a very bad sign. The industry standard is to allow potential members to try before they buy and see if they like the look of the site's members. Anyone who tries to charge you money without showing you the goods has probably got something to hide.

Russian brides and online introduction agencies

If you spend any amount of time looking for dating sites online, you will come across at least a few Russian dating agency sites. Now, before I go any further, I need to point out that I have absolutely nothing against Russian women or Eastern Europeans in general. This is important, as the next thing I am going to say is: avoid these sites at all cost! The whole Russian dating agency thing is a minefield full of scammers, liars and thieves. At best, they are breeding grounds for visa-seekers who are effectively prostituting themselves for a new life in a foreign country. If the worst-case scenario does happen and you get conned out of money, you will have no legal protection whatsoever. The majority of these sites are hosted in places where Internet-related laws are not enforced. Supposedly there are some genuine places out there where at least some of the women are actually looking for love, but I am yet to find any myself. Most agencies display blacklists of women from other agencies, while their own women are in turn blacklisted by their competitors. The safest option is to steer clear and keep to more reputable sites.

A note about the beautiful people

Sometimes, the front page of a site, or the search results might show pictures of men and women who are obviously models, with profiles that are too good to be true. Ever wanted to meet a gorgeous male model-cum-merchant banker who wants to meet women of all ages, shapes and sizes for possible love and marriage? Or how about a female underwear model who loves cooking and cleaning for her man ('looks aren't important')? If these appear too good to be true, it's because they are. In fact, they are fake profiles of people who don't really exist. Usually when this happens, people notice the con straight away (because, let's face it, it's pretty obvious) and assume the site is making up profiles in order to encourage people to join.

While I can't speak for all of the dating sites in the world, I seriously doubt any site does anything of this sort. The fact of the matter is, dating sites are so profitable anyway that there is no need to use such poorly thought out tactics.

These profiles are commonly created by scammers trying to use the sites for their own unwholesome ends. Good sites will be doing everything they can to stop profiles like those from ever appearing but sometimes a few nasties slip through the net. The best thing you can do about such profiles is report them to the site's moderators, who would be happy to remove them.

A fairly incomplete list of popular dating sites

With so many dating sites out there, it would be impossible to list all of them, or even just the good ones. The list below should serve as a starting point and an example of what's out there; it is by no means definitive. I avoided listing niche sites as there are simply too many of them to mention.

Membership prices

The prices below are for a single month's membership. The monthly charges are usually lower for longer membership periods.

Expensive: £30 or more
Standard: £20–£25
Cheap: £10–£20
Very cheap: under £10

General membership sites

These are the big, famous ones. You will have probably heard of some of these already.

DatingDirect

URL: http://www.datingdirect.com

Membership base: varied

General age: any

Sexual preferences catered for: straight or gay. (bisexuals can specify this preference but can't search for both men and women)

Cost: standard

Company location: UK

Features: standard messaging, voice greetings, videos, SMS alerts, singles' events

This is a well-established, functional site, offering a decent package of features. DatingDirect powers many branded dating sites, such as Channel 4 dating, NTLworld dating, etc. and has a very large overall membership base. As far as the online dating experience is concerned, there aren't too many frills here, apart from the addition of handy SMS alerts. The basics are all covered, though, and the site is easy to use and highly popular.

If it were a real-life pick up joint it would be: All Bar One or a similar high-street chain pub

Guardian Soulmates

URL: http://www.guardiansoulmates.com

Membership base: professional, intellectual, left-wing liberal, culturally minded

General age: any

Sexual preferences catered for: any

Cost: standard

Company location: UK

Features: standard messaging, voice clips, basic two-way matching, icebreakers

This offering from the *Guardian* newspaper has become, perhaps unsurprisingly, a highly popular port of call among lefty daters. You don't have to be a *Guardian* reader to date here, but the site has limited appeal for anyone who doesn't share the paper's political and cultural leanings. This makes it instantly exclusive. Guardian Soulmates is a tad text-heavy but is generally well designed and easy to use. It offers some very detailed search options that go beyond those available elsewhere.

If this were a real-life pick up joint it would be: the café at the organic farmers' market or the theatre

Loopylove

URL: http://www.loopylove.com

Membership base: varied

General age: any

Sexual preferences catered for: straight or gay

Cost: standard, free with use of credit system

Company location: UK

Features: standard messaging, chat, multi-user messages, video and voice greetings, SMS alerts, mobile dating

Loopylove's cheap and cheerful approach to online dating has earned it a reputation as a great site for first timers. It's definitely a meat and potatoes sort of place with a very basic, no frills design. In spite of its unassuming look, it offers good value for money, with a large array of features and very detailed search options. Loopylove was the first site in the UK to offer the option of 100% free online dating, although the credit system it employs for this purpose is incredibly annoying to use and generally not worth the hassle.

If it were a real-life pick up joint it would be: your local caff or pub

Match.com

URL: http://uk.match.com/

Membership base: varied

General age: any

Sexual preferences catered for: straight or gay

Cost: standard

Company location: UK branch of US company

Features: standard messaging, icebreakers, basic two-way matching

Match claims to be the biggest online dating company in the world and, whether or not that is true, it is certainly a big, reputable brand. It's clean and sleek to the point of being sterile, which makes it easy to use, although rather lacking in atmosphere. Apart from the usual basic features the site offers a few nice extras. I particularly liked the progress chart that tells you whose turn it is to make the next move and the handy compatibility charts. All in all, this is a reliable, functional site, with much deserved popularity.

If it were a pick up joint it would be: Starbucks

Orientation sites

Jdate

URL: http://www.jdate.com

Membership base: predominantly Jewish, professional

General age: any

Sexual preferences catered for: straight or gay

Cost: standard

Company location: UK branch of US company

Features: standard messaging, chat, icebreakers, e-cards, message boards

Jdate is a big American orientation site aimed at the Jewish community. It has a large UK members' base, as well as sites in France, Canada and Israel. As you'd expect from an American site, it's slick and functional, although the list of features on offer is far from basic. Members can enjoy regular dating events held in cities around the globe. In the UK, they seem to be mostly held in London.

If it were a real life pick up joint it would be: a trendy kosher restaurant

Dating for Parents

URL: http://www.datingforparents.com

Membership base: varied, predominantly single parents

General age: any

Sexual preferences catered for: straight or gay

Cost: standard

Company location: UK

Features: standard messaging, chat, multi-user messages

This site aims to take the sting out of dating as a single parent. All of its members either have children of their own or are open to the possibility of dating people who do. The site offers a basic, yet effective package of features as well as dating and parenting-related articles. It boasts a large membership base and simple functionality that basically does what it says on the box.

If it were a real-life pick up joint it would be: a family pub or a day in the park with the kids

Matching sites

These are sites that offer alternative means of searching for matches. Unlike the basic matching systems offered by other sites, these are rather more complex. For more information about these, see Chapter 5.

DreamsDiscovered

URL: http://www.dreamsdiscovered.com

Membership base: varied, predominantly people looking for serious relationships

General age: any

Sexual preferences catered for: straight or gay

Cost: standard

Company location: UK

Features: standard messaging, chat, multi-user messaging

Members on DreamsDiscovered can actively search for matches as well as make use of a matching system based on a detailed personality test. The personality test was designed by psychologists who specialise in personality assessment for business. It concentrates on factors such as personal goals, motivations and strengths. Members also get a detailed description of their ideal partner's personality and can easily tweak the results to get a different list of matches. Although dry and often grammatically clunky, the test results can be quite insightful. The site is a basic, affordable take on the psychological matching concept.

If it were a real-life pick up joint it would be: a lock and key party

Parship

URL: http://www.parship.co.uk

Membership base: predominantly professional, looking for serious relationships

General age: any

Sexual preferences catered for: straight or gay

Cost: expensive

Company location: UK branch of a German company

Features: Standard messaging, icebreakers, in-depth personality profiling

Behind the warm, trendy exterior that welcomes you to the site hides an incredibly complex matching system.

The test results you get at the end of the 15-20-minutes-long personality testing process are highly detailed and surprisingly accurate. You can even buy a much longer version of the results (80 pages long) if you are so inclined. The site offers no active searching and you must rely entirely on the matching system to provide you with members to speak to. In an attempt to encourage relationships based on factors that are not 'skin deep', the site does not allow you to view photos until you subscribe and even then only at each member's discretion.

If it were a real-life pick up joint it would be: a café designed by Audi

OKcupid

URL: http://www.okcupid.com

Membership base: varied

General age: any

Sexual preferences catered for: any

Cost: free

Company location: USA

Features: standard messaging, chat, blogging, social networking

An American site with a big UK membership base, OKCupid is highly popular, and for a good reason. It manages to be 100% free while still maintaining a high standard, which is an achievement in itself. There are no annoying pop-up ads anywhere and the look and feel are easily as good as any paid site, if not better. The matching system is based on user-submitted questions and a complex algorithm apparently devised by Harvard maths students. It is said to learn and improve the more questions you answer, getting you closer and closer to your perfect match. There are more added all the time, so the process is practically endless. For those not tired of questions, there are plenty of silly personality tests ('which cartoon villain are you?') and other community-enhancing features to keep you entertained.

If it were a real-life pick up joint it would be: a student bar for non-students

Sites with cool concepts

My single friend

URL: http://www.mysinglefriend.com

Membership base: young, trendy, professional, urban, culturally minded

General age: predominantly 18-40

Sexual preferences catered for: any

Cost: cheap

Company location: UK

Features: standard messaging, some social networking

On this site, as the name would suggest, members get their friends to sign them up, write their profiles and leave comments recommending them to others. Everyone you'll find on this site has been effectively pre-vetted by other people, which is a very useful thing. The site is well designed, fun and easy to use, although a bit sparse on the feature front (it seems the only thing you can do on there is send and receive standard messages). The cool concept more than makes up for the site's shortcomings, though, making it one of my personal favourites. Unfortunately, membership can sometimes be sparse outside of certain areas, with rural areas in particular being rather lacking. Hopefully this will change as the site continues to grow.

If it were a real-life pick up joint it would be: a trendy bar or café of the shabby-chic variety

Gorgeous Dating

URL: http://www.gorgeousdating.com

Membership base: professional, trendy, predominantly urban

General age: predominantly 18–35 but some older people too

Sexual preferences catered for: any

Cost: expensive

Company location: UK

Features: standard messaging, singles' events, discounts and freebies to match the 'lifestyle', date coaching, personal introduction services

The Gorgeous Dating team stress that unlike other dating sites, theirs is an exclusive networking club that offers both online and offline services to 'attractive, upwardly mobile, successful single members'. As a dating site, it has basic, sometimes clunky functionality, but more than makes up for it with its community feel and the personal attention given to its members. It feels more like a private social club than a standard dating site: members must be voted in and are then encouraged to attend frequent singles' parties and events. Flirty and fun, this is a good site for people who enjoy painting the town red.

If it were a real-life pick up joint it would be: the café at an exclusive health club, if it served champagne cocktails

Chapter 3

Your profile and you

In this chapter you will find out about:

■ Setting up your profile

■ The makings of a good profile

■ Things to avoid when writing a profile

Make yourself stand out

On any decent dating site there are plenty of other people trying to find love. You will need to make yourself stand out if you want people to notice you. When people decide whether or not to contact someone they do it very quickly: sometimes within seconds. You will be doing the exact same things yourself when you come to choose your own potential dates.

You may have heard that the picture is the only thing anyone ever looks at, but that is not strictly true. Yes, everyone looks at the pictures first, which is why I've allocated the next chapter to discussing them. However, what you write in your profile can still make a world of difference. We all know that not everyone in the world is photogenic and people often make allowances for that. If your profile shows character, it could count for a lot more than you might think. A bad profile, however, could put people off even the most attractive person.

This chapter is all about coming up with good stuff to write about yourself so you can make your profile work for you, rather than against you.

Setting up your profile

You set up the profile when you join a site and the procedure varies in length and complexity from one site to another. Sometimes the process is short and straightforward and sometimes it's very long and drawn out, full of lengthy personality tests or page after page of questions. Usually, the registration process will involve choosing a username and then answering a set of multiple-choice questions. You will then get a chance to write a bit of blurb about yourself and what you are looking for, as well as any interests, hobbies etc.

Placeholders

You may well not like the thought of having to set up your profile before being allowed to search the site. Nobody likes filling out forms, answering heaps of questions and writing essays, especially when all you really want to do is look at other people's profiles.

This is why a lot of people rush through the registration process by putting some kind of non-committal placeholder in place. This usually involves writing something along the lines of 'I'll tell you later' instead of an actual description and maybe even skipping some questions along the way. Doing this may seem like a good idea when all you want to do is cut to the chase, but really it's not so great. The profile is the best way for you to show others what your personality is like and make them want to get to know you. Cut corners here, and you may find yourself at a distinct disadvantage later on.

When you send a message to someone on a site, the first thing he will do is check out your profile. If the profile is good, he may choose to reply to even the most uninspired message because your profile would tell him you are not really a bore.

A bad profile could mean you will never get contacted. The only exceptions to this rule are beautiful women who get contacted all the time regardless of their profile text. I'll let you be the judge of the quality of responses one can get based on a good picture alone. Suffice it to say, the men who contact such women are not interested in their conversation skills.

If you are following my advice in the previous chapter and are just looking around a site to decide whether you want to join it, there is no need to bother writing up a good profile just yet. A placeholder of some kind is more than enough to get you signed up and searching. If, on the other hand, you want to actually meet and speak to people, you will need to create a proper profile and put some thought into it.

Remember: Your profile defines you to potential partners. They have no other way of knowing who you are. Every single bit of information you put in it counts, because when choosing to include it, you are saying that you see it as important.

Men scan, women read

As I mentioned above, both men and women check out the pictures first when browsing profiles. However, research has shown that men and women are very different when it comes to reading the text on a page. It turns out that men usually scan the page, picking out bits of information quickly, whereas women generally spend a bit more time reading the full text. There is no need for me to bore you with any theories about why this could be.

Instead, you can use this information to help you write your profile in a way that will be more accessible to your target audience.

- If you are a woman looking for men, you should keep your sentences short and to the point, delivering a single bit of information in each. Avoid long, rambling sentences and long anecdotes. Put the most important information about you and your requirements at the beginning of the profile and work your way down to less important things. If a man is interested in you he will read the whole profile, but you need to get his attention first.

- If you are a man, remember that women generally read the full text of the profile before deciding whether or not to contact someone. Make sure you write enough information about yourself to make things interesting. A couple of lines of text won't really cut it.

Your objectives

In contrast to social networking sites (e.g., Myspace.com), community sites etc., a personal profile on a dating site has only two objectives.

The profile is there to:

- Tell people about you and what you're looking for
- Make people want to get to know you better (i.e. reply to your messages or contact you of their own accord)

While it's easy to write an informative profile, it's also easy to forget about the second objective and include information that is unnecessary and even damaging. Always remember that the purpose of the profile is to 'sell' you to potential matches. The 'sale' in this case means making the other person want to contact you. Everything you put in your profile must therefore be geared towards meeting *both* the above objectives, not just the first one.

Obviously, presenting a good profile doesn't mean lying to cover up things you think are not attractive, but working with what you have in order to show *your* best side.

Building a good profile from the ground up

Before we get into all the stuff about writing a profile, here's a quick word of advice. On the Internet, where it's hard to figure out what a person is like, little things matter more than you might think. In fact, it's sometimes those little things that can cause the biggest problems.

Your username

In my moderating days I occasionally came across some beautifully written profiles of both men and women describing themselves as hopeless romantics and saying they were looking for their soulmates. Unfortunately, their usernames were things like 'sexyslut' or 'sexaddict2000', which painted a slightly different picture. As you can probably guess, these people didn't do very well on the sites and were more than a bit disappointed. For all I know, those poorly chosen usernames could have been chosen as a joke and were no indication of anything other than a keen sense of humour. Sadly, irony is usually lost online. Using humour is great, but make sure you use a joke that can't be taken the wrong way otherwise people might think you really mean it. Choose your username wisely.

The tag line

Most sites give you the opportunity to provide a short caption, headline, chat up line, or *tag line* that will appear in a prominent place in your profile (such as above or under your picture). This line can also sometimes appear with your picture in search results and so may end up being one of the first parts of your profile that people see.

Regardless of the name given to this line by the site you are using, you are free to use it as you see fit. Don't feel obliged to use it to describe your picture, even if the site has named this line a caption. Think of it as a headline or a 'teaser' – something to make people want to read the rest of your profile.

Newspaper editors know that you can sell more papers with an enticing headline than by giving away the whole story in the title of an article. Withholding details arouses people's curiosity and they are then more likely to buy a copy of the paper. Similarly, you don't have to overstuff *your* headline/tag line with details about yourself. Save that stuff for the rest of the profile where it belongs. What you are trying to do here is attract attention and give people a brief idea of the kind of person you are.

For some people, this will be an easy exercise, while others find this kind of thing more difficult than writing long essays. If you're finding it difficult, don't worry too much about it. Unless you write something offensive, you are not likely to put anyone off with a less-than-perfect tag line.

The makings of a good tag line

- Humour sells: short jokes, silly comments, bad chat up lines, anything that puts a smile on your face is good.

- A short bit of text that sums up who you are or what you are looking for makes a simple, yet effective tag line; just remember not to write too much.

- Movie quotes and song lyrics may not be the most original thing in the world, but they can certainly sum things up nicely and show people what you like.

Examples:

> *'Free your mind and the rest will follow'*
>
> *'Friendly northern lad looking for some fun'*
>
> *'What did the chicken say to the duck?'*
>
> *'Fancy a drink?'*
>
> *'You do know how to whistle, don't you?'*

Tag lines that will make you look bad

- Overly suggestive comments (unless you really are only looking for sex)

- Anything that makes it look like you couldn't be bothered to think of something good to write

- Lines that get cut off half way because you ran out of space

- Personal information that belongs in the longer part of the profile

Examples:

> *'Horny babe, up for anything!'*
> *'I don't know what to write here'*
> *'If you are ever in the Manchester area give me a ri'*
> *'I am 44, work as a legal secretary and have blue eyes'*

Tick boxes, multiple-choice questions and lists

Dating sites know how much people hate filling out forms and a lot of them try to simplify the process by asking you questions and providing tick boxes for things like interests, hobbies etc. These can be very useful but also a bit limiting at times. The amount of such questions you will be asked depends on the site you are using.

When answering the questions, be as honest as possible. It's usually better to tell the truth from the beginning, as most lies are exposed very early on. The questions people are most likely to lie about are age, body type and marital status, so we'll look at those first.

Age

Although it's generally good to be honest, this is the one exception where sometimes it's OK to lie. This is particularly true for women and more so if the site you are on divides people into age groups in the search criteria. Women who look younger than their age are at a distinct disadvantage online, where people define their search by specifying numbers. If you are the sort of person who always gets surprised looks when you reveal your age, you may want to consider lowering your age slightly in order to appear in more searches. This is especially important if you are a woman over 50, or fall just outside a specified age group. If you do lie, make sure you refer to this in your description section and explain why you did it. You don't want to lead people on for too long, or they will get angry.

If you are used to social networking sites (such as MySpace.com), forums, etc., you may be tempted to sign up with a joke age such as 99 or 100. On dating sites, this is a very bad idea, as it would mean you would hardly show up in any searches. Either use your real age or lie as explained above.

Body type

Many people are tempted to lie about this, especially if they are a bit over-weight and are working towards losing the extra pounds.

Of course, any lies about personal appearance would be quickly exposed on the first date, which is the event you are basically working towards. Be truthful about your appearance, and use the description area too if you want to let people know you are working out. Once you've lost the extra pounds, you can change your profile to match.

Marital status

If you are separated, say that you are separated rather than divorced. If the site doesn't offer that as an option, use 'divorced' and explain the situation in the profile. Nothing annoys people more than being lied to about someone's marital status. As we all know, there are plenty of people out there who are married and choose to cheat on their spouses. If you've bought this book then hopefully I can assume you are not one of them. However, if you are, be aware that there are some dating sites out there that cater specifically for married/attached people who wish to cheat. There are also sites for swingers and those in open marriages/relationships who are open to the concept of consensual extra-marital sex. There really is no need to lie. Occasionally, even daters on general membership sites will openly admit to being married and looking to cheat on their spouse without suffering any adverse conse-quences. Moral implications aside, I see this as a welcome change, as it means people can make more informed decisions about the relationships they choose to enter.

More tips about answering questions

Most sites will let you opt out of answering questions that you don't feel comfortable answering. If you don't want to answer something and can't opt out, choose a false answer, but make sure you mention that in your descrip-tion. The only exceptions to this are the age question (where choosing a joke age would be a bad idea) and the postcode. This is because most people search by age or distance and you want them to be able to find you. You can generally get around limiting multiple-choice questions or tick boxes by picking the closest answer and clarifying things in your description.

Lists of interests etc. often have a format you need to conform to, but it is not always clear what that format is. Some expect you to input words or phrases separated by commas and get confused if you don't, making everything you've written look weird. Always check your profile when you have finished, to make sure everything is as it should be.

The personal blurb

The personal blurb is where you get to talk about yourself in your own words. The people who read your profile will use this information to try and figure out what you're like. Put thought into what you write, as every little bit counts towards making people want to know you better. You have complete control over what goes into your profile and so, in effect, complete control over how you will appear to others online.

The personal description is the hardest part for most people to write, so don't worry if the perfect bit of text fails to miraculously flow through your fingers straight away. With very few exceptions, there is no such thing as effortlessly good writing. Those charming profiles that flow so naturally probably took ages to write and perfect. Don't judge your first effort by such end results. If your initial attempt seems to lack that award-winning quality you hoped for, all is not lost. There are ways and means of getting over the profile hurdle and writing something you'll be happy with. Most importantly: take your time and view everything you do as a work in progress.

Checking out the competition

Just because you are a man looking for a woman or a woman looking for a man, doesn't mean you can't run a quick search on the site and examine those you are competing against for the opposite sex's attention. Looking at the prevalent profiles on your site will allow you to spot clichés more easily so you can avoid them in your own writing. Don't try and match your profile to others you may find on the site: you are trying to stand out, not fit in!

How much to write

Opinions vary as to how much you should put in a profile. The general rule is that you should write enough for people to get the information they need but not so much that they get bored and stop reading. Usually, this means writing around 200–300 words, though I've seen some good profiles that were shorter. Different sites structure their user profiles differently and so this limit is flexible. Some sites have different text boxes for a list of hobbies/interests and some even offer separate boxes for things such as favourite music, films etc. In such cases, your best bet would be to keep the main essay relatively short and fill out the respective text boxes separately. On sites that don't provide such distinction, you can afford to write a longer profile with all those items incorporated into one body of text. Even on sites like this, writing much over 300 words in one box is usually a waste of time, as most people won't bother reading that far.

The structure of a good profile

A good profile needs to include the following information:

- A description of you, both physical and non-physical: character traits; likes/dislikes; hobbies and interests; hopes, dreams and/or past achievements and anything else you think may be relevant to your personality
- Information about what you would bring to the relationship
- A description of what you are looking for in a partner

The above is not a formula that should be followed in a particular order or fashion but general guidelines for the sort of information you should weave into the profile in whatever order suits you. This is the sort of information people want to get when they read profiles.

On some sites, you will have already answered some of these questions using a tick box or smaller text box and there is no need to repeat such information in the essay part or write a long profile for the sake of it. Use that space instead to fill in the gaps and expand on that information, or write about entirely different aspects of yourself.

Tricks and tips for writing

A dry run
Have you ever written a birthday card for someone and struggled to come up with something clever to write? I know I have, but I've found that I could think more clearly if I started by writing out my ideas on another

piece of paper first, when I didn't have to worry about making a mess of it. Typing your profile into the text box provided by your dating site can sometimes feel oddly 'final'. To make things easier, it's best to write the personal description somewhere else first. Personally, I like using a word processing package like Microsoft Word, because it makes editing simple. I can then cut and paste the result every time I sign up to a new site, thus saving me the trouble of writing a new profile each time. This also gives me the time I need to come up with whatever it is I want to write without worrying about making mistakes or having the site timeout on me.

If you are one of those people who hate typing and find it a lot easier to write with pen and paper, there is no reason why you shouldn't do that first and then type your text in when you're ready. The goal here is to get you in the mood to do your best writing. How you do it is entirely up to you.

Expressing yourself

Back in the old days, people used to spend a lot more time writing about personal things. Long, involved letters to friends and family were very common then, but have mostly been replaced by phone calls now. Even when we use emails, we usually keep them brief and chatty. For most of us, writing about ourselves is done only in a professional context. This form of writing is generally drier and requires that we disregard any emotional issues (as they are largely irrelevant). As a result, many of us have now lost the ability to comfortably express our feelings in writing.

While researching this book I found that usually one of two things happens when a person not used to writing about himself sits down in front of a computer and attempts to do it. The first is being completely blocked and unable to write a single word: like an animal caught in the headlights. The second thing is exactly the opposite: the act of writing acts as a release and words flow quite naturally, almost uncontrollably. If you are one of those lucky people who can just sit down and let everything out – you're doing well. The important thing for you is to make sure you read over everything you've written and remove anything that doesn't do you justice. More often than not, people write their profile in haste and the result is a sort of stream of consciousness containing things that should really be left out of a dating profile.

Never allow yourself to be defined by a negative stream of consciousness when you can easily control the information you provide.

What information to include

Imagine you are meeting someone at a party for the first time. What would you like to know about that person? What questions would you ask? Those are the questions you should answer in your own profile.

If you are finding it hard to think of any questions, you can use the ones below as a guide. You can also refer back to the questions at the end of Chapter 1. Obviously, you can choose to answer as many or as few of them as you like, or not use them at all. Writing a profile is a personal thing, after all.

- What hobbies and activities do you enjoy?
- What past achievements are you most proud of?
- What are your hopes for the future?
- Have you ever visited any exciting places?
- What places would you like to visit?
- What is your favourite food?
- What is your sense of humour like?
- What are you like with your friends?
- What are you like with your other half when in a relationship?
- What sort of person are you looking for?
- What sort of music/films/TV shows do you like?
- What do you do for a living?

Being honest without shooting yourself in the foot

Because of the direct nature of online dating, where people can specify all those deal breakers straight away, there is a temptation to lay all the cards on the table from the beginning and prevent future misunderstandings. Unfortunately, there is a fine line between being honest and being *too* honest. There is no point being in a relationship where you have to be on your best behaviour all the time, but at such an early stage, when you are trying to attract someone's attention for the first time, some things can and should be left out of your profile. It is your profile that defines you to other people online. What do *you* want to be defined by?

What's 'normal'?

Alternative lifestyle choices, any piercings and tattoos you may have and any unusual professions or hobbies you enjoy can and should be included in your profile. There is no need to be ashamed of who you are and what you love and no need to put on a 'normal' face to the world if that is not *your* face. Things like bad habits, bad break-ups, general dissatisfaction with life, etc., on the other hand, can and should be left out.

A personal cover letter

A good way of thinking about the profile is to compare it to the cover letter that accompanies your CV when you apply for a job. When writing a cover letter you would most likely choose to concentrate on your past achievements and current motivations as well as the good qualities and experience you would bring to the role you are applying for. If your CV has any problems, you may use your cover letter to address them ('the reason for the gap between my last job and the current one is that I took maternity leave in order to have my son').

It's safe to assume that you would avoid mentioning anything bad that may damage your chances of getting the job ('my last employer told me I had a problem with authority – so I told him where to shove it'). While writing with such honesty would indeed tell your potential employers everything they need to know about you, it would probably not get you the job.

Similarly, when writing for people who may want to date you, it's best to concentrate on your attractive qualities and leave out anything negative for the time being.

This is why it's important to be in a positive frame of mind when writing the profile, as any negative feelings you may have about yourself and/or the opposite sex could show through and may put people off.

The example below shows what I mean:

> 'I am a 45-year-old woman, a single mother with two wonderful children (one still living at home). I love my job and my friends and am looking for a man to complete the picture. I've had a few really bad experiences with men lately and I am wondering whether I am losing my faith in mankind! I feel so lonely sometimes but also angry about the way some men treat women. I really want to find a man who will treat me right for a change and not just use me. My last boyfriend took off with some of my money and would have probably taken all of it if I didn't stop him. I think most men are users. There has to be someone there for me who isn't? Maybe it's just me picking the wrong guys. I hope so, or I am in big trouble!'

This woman started with good intentions, but then the pain and frustration of being alone and recovering from a string of bad break-ups took over and she had to let it out. The message she is now sending out is that she has a lot of issues to deal with that may affect how she acts in a relationship. Any man reading her profile would be wary of contacting her, as she seems so mistrustful and bitter. In reality, the woman could be very kind and trusting, but starting to write about herself could have triggered an emotional response that touched on a bad place. This is exactly why writing is such a good tool for working through pain and unresolved issues. However, this example shows why you should be careful when writing your profile. If you have such feelings you want to share with others online, I would suggest a blog, a social networking site or an online support group. These are all great tools for working through issues and maybe even getting support. Leave your dating profile to do what it's meant to do: present you in a positive manner to people who may want to go out with you. Had the woman in the example above stopped to read her profile critically, she would have realised she had included information in it that is unhelpful to her dating 'career'.

If in doubt when writing your own profile, refer back to the questions at the end of Chapter 1, which should help you assess your current state of mind. If you can't write anything positive truthfully, it may be wise to wait until you can so that you can get the most out of your dating experience.

Things that make a good profile

Think positive

Talk about things that make you feel good about your life right now – hobbies, your job, time spent with friends, your last holiday, etc. There is nothing wrong with explaining why you are single and looking for love online, of course, but wallowing in self-pity will not help you in your quest.

When talking about the type of people you want to meet, it's good practice to say what you want, rather than what you don't want – especially when it comes to matters of physical build, ethnicity and religion. I have come across some profiles of men who'd written stuff like 'no fat chicks' when listing their requirements. All that does is make those men look like jerks. Even fit women wouldn't want to contact such men. Why not say you are looking for someone athletic instead? It says the same thing without being insulting. We cannot help what qualities we find attractive, but it helps to be sensitive when pointing such things out to others.

Be particularly wary of using lines like 'no gold-diggers', which would instantly make people think you are tight with money.

Phrases like 'no time wasters, please' may seem like a good idea for nipping unwanted attention in the bud but actually have very little meaning. It would be better to give an explanation of what you view as a waste of time, e.g., 'please don't contact me if you are only looking for sex, I want a serious relationship!'

Other cases where it is acceptable to use negative phrasing and talk about what you *don't* want are when talking about people's vices (i.e. 'no smokers, please') or when saying that you want to meet people who don't have children. Even in such cases, it helps to respect others' lifestyle choices rather than blatantly slag them off.

Use humour

Everyone loves a laugh so feel free to be funny. Even a random joke you like can work well in a profile, as long as you include some personal information in there as well.

You don't need to try too hard to think of something that would make other people laugh. If something makes *you* laugh it will make a similar-minded person laugh too, which is all you should really care about. If you have an obscure sense of humour, some people may be put off by your jokes, but who cares; would you really want to go out with such people anyway? As long as you make sure none of your jokes can be seen as offensive, you have nothing to worry about.

Get friends and family to help

Nowadays, when the stigma associated with online dating is practically gone, it's becoming more and more common for people to share their profiles with friends and family and ask for advice. This is a good way of getting a second opinion and they can even help you come up with a description of your character.

Ask your friends what they would say about you if they were setting you up on a blind date and your date wanted to know what you were like. You can even ask them to talk about times you've shared together that they thought are particularly representative of your character.

Be descriptive

Many people start writing about themselves and end up producing a long list of adjectives without going any further. Adjectives mean different things to different people, which is why they are more or less useless on their own. It's easy to write, 'I'm funny' but harder to make someone laugh. One person's idea of humour could send someone else into fits of boredom. How would anyone know if your ideas of humour are the same?

Using clichés such as 'up for a laugh', 'genuine' and 'off the wall' is also an easy way out that would leave your readers in the dark. It's like writing in code and expecting the person on the other side to be using the same key as you in order to crack it.

As a rule, it's always best to show people what you are like, rather than tell them. When writers write fiction, they show the readers what a character is like by writing about the character's actions. Want to show someone as being generous? Write about him donating half his fortune to charity. Want to expose a villain? Write about his evil exploits. In your profile, you could similarly use personal anecdotes or visual descriptions to show your readers what you are like.

You don't need to be a poet to be descriptive. It's actually very simple to go beyond empty adjectives. Write out the words you think sum you up best (romantic, caring, silly, up for anything) and then start asking yourself: 'what do I mean by that?' Keep doing it until you are satisfied that what you've written is clear and leaves no room for questions.

Did you say you are up for anything? What did you mean by that? Are you the sort of person who never says no to a dare? If so, what was the craziest thing you've ever done on a dare? Do you like trying new things? What was the best thing you tried recently, or the worst?

Did you say you are romantic? What did you mean by that? Do you like giving or receiving flowers? Do you like rainy days or cuddling on the sofa when it's cold? Do you write poetry?

All these things will give your potential dates a much better glimpse at your personality than merely coding all that information into a single word and expecting them to know what you mean.

Things that make a bad profile

In my experience, it's very easy to do yourself an injustice when writing the profile. I have come across many generous, well-adjusted people (by anyone's standards) whose profiles made them appear far less appealing. The reason behind this is more often than not a misunderstanding of how the profile may look to a stranger. We all know ourselves pretty well, certainly well enough to know what we mean by the words we say. Unfortunately, this is not always the case when these words are the only information people have about us. Here are some common things that would make you look bad online.

Giving out personal details
A lot of people try to get around paying for membership by including things like phone numbers and email addresses in their profiles.

Apart from making you look cheap, this is also likely to get the site owners angry (possibly angry enough to remove your profile), as well as potentially putting you at risk. Online safety will be discussed in more detail in Chapter 8.

Being too modest

There is a fine line between modesty and self-deprecation. I have seen far too many people describe themselves as 'normal' and 'average' as well as 'not much to look at' and 'nothing special'. The worst ones are things along the lines of 'I may not be Brad Pitt, but…' or 'I may not be a work of art, but…'. Using lines like these would only set you up for failure. Never use your profile to apologise for your looks. You may think you are showing modesty and a healthy awareness of your flaws but the only thing you will achieve by such detractions is showing people you are insecure. The photo you upload should tell people what you look like; people don't need you to explain it to them. Let them make their minds up about whether or not they fancy you.

You should only ever refer to yourself as average if you are of average build. Unless you are describing your build, using the word 'average' only means one thing: boring. If you think you are boring, why should anyone else be interested in meeting you? Instead of attempting to describe yourself with adjectives, talk about stuff that you do and stuff that you want to do. Let the reader decide if that's 'average'. A hobby or profession you may think is common and unimpressive may really fascinate people if you let them know about it.

Being too arrogant

Another fine line is that between confidence and arrogance. It's great to have things to be proud of in our lives but nobody likes a show-off. Don't ever describe yourself as 'attractive' or 'hot': let people make their own minds up in the same way you would if you thought you were plain. Vanity is not an attractive quality in anyone and is a sure way of putting people off. As for your other good qualities, there is no need to avoid mentioning them: it's those qualities that will get people interested in you. You may, however, need to tone things down a bit to make yourself sound modest, as well as cool.

Compare the following two profile segments:

> I work out 5 days a week and I reckon I am the fittest guy at my gym. I can give anyone a run for their money; I am simply the best and there's no two ways about it!

> I may not be Jean Claude Van Damme but I do work out 5 days a week and consider myself to be in very good shape. I would go as far as saying I am the fittest guy at my gym, but you might think I am a bit full of myself then!

Using detractions and self-deprecating humour in this case is a good way of toning down an otherwise rather showy statement. The difference is subtle but important.

Disproportionate profiles

It's worth keeping in mind that any aspect of your life you go into in your profile at depth or make a point of mentioning, will translate in the mind of the reader into something you think is important and/or attractive. For example, going on at length about how much money you earn will make people think you place a lot of importance on money issues. Making a big deal of how fit/beautiful you are will make people think you place a lot of importance on looks. Go too far and people will think you are obsessed.

If you only write about a particular aspect of your life, you may attract people who only care about that particular aspect because you have neglected to mention any of your other qualities. That is why people who write about their income, for example, end up with gold-diggers. If you want people to show interest in you and not your money, don't tell them how much you earn until you get to know them better. Use your other fine qualities to attract them in the first instance.

A list of demands

Sometimes, people don't give any information about themselves but only include information of their requirements. I once saw a profile where a man had written half a page about the physical characteristics he wanted in his ideal partner. He was very specific, noting measurements, hair and eye colour and even ideal shoe size (!).

Personally, I found that profile creepy, as it seemed as if the man was interested in nothing else but looks. It sounded like he'd written down some kind of sexual fantasy or was trying to acquire a mail-order bride. Such a profile is sending the message that the man is really only interested in sex with a particular type of woman. Sadly for him, I doubt any woman would want to contact him based on *that* profile!

Here is another example from a woman's profile:

> I want to meet a man who is kind and caring, over 5′11″. He needs to be honest and genuine and like cats and children.

Apart from the adjective problem already discussed (what does she mean by 'genuine?) the other question that should be asked is: why would the tall, caring, genuine guy want to contact this woman?

It's not enough to tell people what you want, you need to explain to them what they will get in return:

> I am a friendly person who's always there for friends and family when needed. I work for a children's charity and also volunteer at the local homeless shelter. I am into photography, especially portraits, as I love working with people. I enjoy beach holidays in the sun, doesn't everyone??? I am quite tall, 5′10′ and so would really like to find a man who is at least 5′1I′. I have a daughter who is 7 and wonderful and also a cat. I am looking for someone who would love us all and is honest and genuine.

This profile doesn't just give a clearer idea of this person, it also explains why she wants what she wants. You don't always need to explain why you are attracted to a particular type of person but the more demanding you are of your ideal partner, the more you should make sure you mention your own fine qualities in return.

Accusing tone
Here is an example of a profile that is not likely to attract much interest:

I have given up on all women because I think they are all out to cheat men and just want to take their money and run. Maybe you could be the one to prove me wrong?

Statements like this one always take me back to my school days. Remember those stern, nasty teachers who would walk into class and make you feel guilty even though you hadn't done anything wrong? Reading the profile above would immediately make me look back at my last relationship and wonder whether I had paid for enough dinners. Was I out to cheat my ex out of his hard earned cash? Am I a bad woman like all those others out there?

Instead of making anyone rise to the challenge, accusations like that will only get people's backs up. Suspicion and mistrust are not qualities we want in a relationship, especially when you've never even met the person. Why would I want to prove something to a person I have never met? Why would I want to meet someone who thinks all women are cheats? No, thank you.

Crowd-pleasing

Don't think that you have to make up exciting stuff about yourself or your life in order to attract people. Saying you are a lion-tamer, a secret agent or the Queen of England may get you a few responses, but unless you are who you claim to be, you will find your new friends' interest levels drop very quickly when they find out you were lying. There is no need to present yourself as someone you are not. After all, you want to meet people who will find you appealing for who you really are.

Offensive/sexual language

For some reason, some people choose to include graphic descriptions of their favourite sexual acts, boasts about their sexual prowess and similar things of this sort. This is generally deemed unacceptable behaviour and would put most people off anyway.

Different sites have different moderation policies and language that is acceptable on one site may be inappropriate on another. As a general rule, though, unless you are on an openly sexually oriented site, you will be expected to keep things pretty clean.

'Just looking'

Even if you are just trying out a site, there is no reason to tell people that in the profile. Telling people you are just having a look around will stop anyone from contacting you. They will assume you're hardly ever there and are not likely to respond to any messages they send. If you want people to take the time to contact you, make them think it will be worth their while.

Chapter 4

Your picture

In this chapter you will find out about:

■ Why you should upload a picture

■ How to upload a picture

■ Choosing a good picture

■ What different pictures say about you

Why upload a picture?

If you are serious about trying online dating, you will absolutely have to upload a picture. Being camera-shy myself, I can sympathise with anyone who's put off by the idea, but there is no escape. The fact of the matter is that unless you are willing to show your face to the online world, you may as well hang up your mouse and keyboard and give up on the whole thing right now.

Some people are unpleasantly surprised when their dreams of complete online anonymity fail to materialise. If you were hoping to make a connection online based solely on the power of your personality, you too will most likely be disappointed. There are still places on the Internet where it is acceptable for people to get to know each other without sharing pictures, but those are usually places not designed specifically for dating. On dating sites, where the ultimate goal is an actual relationship, people want to see the goods very early on.

There are, of course, some exceptions (like parship.co.uk), where you can opt to release your photos only to certain individuals, but those are few and far between (partly because there isn't much demand for them).

Even if you are unhappy with your physical appearance, it's better to let people see what you look like than let them imagine the worst. This is why, in most cases, even an unflattering photo is preferable to no photo at all. Most online daters will not bother contacting someone whose profile doesn't have at least one picture. If they come across a profile like that, they will most likely ignore it and move on. Some sites even let their members opt out of viewing profiles that don't contain photos. If you thought about compromising by sending your picture to interested parties by email, think again: most people wouldn't even know you existed unless you uploaded one in the first place.

'But there are many perfectly valid reasons why I may not want to upload a photo' I can hear you say, and you are absolutely right. I have come across many doctors, psychologists and teachers who didn't want any of their patients/students finding them dating on the Internet. Unfortunately, as far as the average online dater is concerned, not having a photo is a bad sign.

Instead of stopping to think about what may have caused a person to choose such anonymity, the majority of daters will suspect foul play of some sort. That is, of course, if they bother looking at the profile in the first place.

Do looks really matter online?

I'll start with the bad news: your photo will be the first thing people will look at when they view your profile. It may even be the thing that makes them view your profile in the first place. There is nothing sinister about this, the human eye is naturally drawn to the image of the human face. Even advertisers know this, which is why so many companies use pictures of people among their advertising blurb. Saying that, there is no use pretending that looks don't matter online.

When you start dating on the Internet, you will be checking out people's pictures to see whether or not you are attracted to them. Other people in turn will check you out in much the same way. You may think that is a shallow way of looking at things, but I believe it's perfectly understandable. Luckily, not all of us are looking for the same thing, so someone you find attractive would be very different from another person's ideal match. People come in all shapes and sizes and are attracted to people in all shapes and sizes. Instead of being worried about looks and beauty standards, concentrate on finding a picture that shows you in your best light and leave the rest to the eye of the beholder.

Uploading your picture

Usually, uploading a picture is a pretty straightforward procedure. You will need to have your picture digitised and it will need to be in keeping with the specifications listed on the site. You will then be able to upload it to the website using your browser. Most sites have an upper size limit for photos, which you will need to comply with. If your picture is too big, you will need to resize it using image editing software.

If you have trouble uploading the picture, some sites let you email it to them or even post them a copy so that they can then digitise it for you. In the UK, it's sometimes possible to send photos via your mobile phone.

Most sites will have a moderation policy for pictures and your picture (or even your profile) may be removed if you break any of the rules. Make sure you read the rules before you upload anything, so that you know what you can and can't do. On most moderated sites you may find there is a time delay between the moment you upload your picture and the moment it appears on your profile. This is because each photo has to be viewed by a moderator before being allowed on the site. How long this takes varies between sites, but you will usually get a message letting you know how long you should expect to wait. Needless to say, uploading your picture ten times because it didn't appear instantly won't make this process any quicker.

Your objectives

Much like the written profile, a picture on a dating site has only two objectives. Perhaps unsurprisingly, those objectives are pretty similar to the ones relating to your profile.

Your photo is there in order to:

■ Show people what you look like

■ Make potential matches want to contact you

The information a picture sends needs to be separated into the two distinct parts. The first part is your physical appearance. The second is what the picture says about your personality. This can be found in your choice of clothing, where the picture was taken, what you are doing in the picture etc. Obviously, if you use a simple headshot, you won't have too many other details to worry about.

Women try harder

A woman I know who runs a popular dating site, conducted some research and found that men and women often differ in the way they choose their profile pictures. Women usually put more thought into the pictures they choose, some even opting to have makeovers and professional photo sessions. Men, on the other hand, often pick whatever picture they have handy and slap it on their profile.

It turns out that women who agree to go on dates with men whose pictures aren't that great, are often pleasantly surprised. Some men, however, are actually disappointed when the women they meet in real life fail to live up to their online image.

So what can be learnt from this?

■ Men should choose their photos more carefully, as they may be missing out on dates by uploading poor photos. If you are a man, you may want to consider getting a female friend to help you choose a good photo, as this would give you a different perspective.

■ Women should make sure at least some of the photos they pick represent what they look like in everyday life. While a makeover can be a great confidence-booster, it's not really necessary to try that hard. In fact, looking like you're trying too hard can actually end up working against you.

Taking pictures

You can usually get great results by asking a friend or relative to take your picture. Ideally, you want to show the world what you look like in more casual circumstances. You could pick a time when you are out and wearing your party clothes or even dress up especially for the occasion and have the photos taken at home or another location that appeals to you. Pick a location that's well lit, somewhere that makes you feel comfortable and relaxed. If possible, use a digital camera, so that you can take plenty of pictures until you get one that you like. Try to avoid taking pictures of yourself, especially if you only have a web camera or a phone camera. Such pictures are hardly ever flattering. In all cases: smile!

Good pictures, bad pictures and how to choose

A friend's advice

If you already have pictures you want to use, get a friend or relative to help you choose your picture if you can. It's good to have a second opinion, especially if you generally don't like having your picture taken.

Show yourself

You can choose any picture, not necessarily one that was taken especially for the purpose of being uploaded to a dating site. Often, though, pictures taken with a dating profile in mind end up being the most flattering ones. A good picture for a dating site is one that shows you clearly. Most dating sites won't even allow you to upload a picture that doesn't show your face, let alone one that isn't of you at all. Some sites will let you upload more than one picture and are a bit more forgiving about what you can use as your additional photos but that is not always the case. As a rule, a picture on a dating site is not there to show people who you are metaphorically, it's there to show people what you *actually* look like. Pictures of cartoon characters, your favourite actor, your pets or your child's drawings are not suitable for the purposes of online dating.

Show your face

Your main picture should always be one where your face is showing clearly. Full body shots are great, as long as your face is still clearly visible. Otherwise, upload the full body shot as your second image and get a headshot done first.

Keep it simple

Simple works best. There is no need for busy backgrounds, exotic locations or anything else that may detract from the main attraction: you. Pick a shot where you are smiling and look happy. People will forgive a lot in terms of appearance if the person in the photo looks like someone who knows how to have a laugh.

Up to date

The picture you choose should be a recent one where you look like you do in real life right now. It may be tempting to pick a photo from ten years ago when you had a bit more hair or were a few pounds lighter, but sooner or later the truth will have to come out. Letting people develop false expectations will only work against you in the long run. Showing people who you really are will mean that you will only get contacted by people who actually find you attractive.

Just you ...

A good photo is one of you on your own. Photos of you with your mates, etc. are too confusing because people will not know who's who. Also, dating sites may not let you upload such photos, fearing prosecution from irate non-members featured on the site against their will.

... not your ex-partner

There is no excuse in the world that would justify uploading a picture of you with your ex, absolutely none, ever. I've seen people who actually uploaded their own wedding photos, taking care to cut their ex husband/ wife's face out of the frame. I can only guess that this was meant innocently enough, in order to make use of what they saw as a decent picture of themselves. Of course, I could be wrong: they could have actually *wanted* to make themselves look like complete nutters. Don't do it. Even a scanned passport photo would be better than something like that.

... or your children

Never upload photos of your children or of you with your children. Most sites won't even allow this in the first place for legal reasons. Adult dating and children are two concepts that should be kept separate, even on sites that cater specifically to single parents.

Keep your clothes on

I know that it goes without saying that uploading naked pictures of yourself is a very bad idea (it does go without saying, right?) but any pictures with plenty of skin showing can work against you, even if they are not suggestive or sexual in nature. Bikini shots, Speedo shots, just-out-of-the-shower shots – any photos where you are blatantly more naked than not – are going to make people think that you are offering sex. Obviously, if you're dating on a sex site, then all bets are off: point your web camera down at the goods and off you go. On all other sites, think hard before using your physical assets as your main selling point. I have seen far too many profiles of women where the text spoke about wanting to find a serious relationship but the photo showed mostly cleavage. The only messages these women are ever going to get are ones asking for sex. It doesn't matter what their profiles say, no man would ever stop to read them.

> **Remember:** if you use only your body to attract people, you will attract people who are only interested in your body.

Different pictures and what they say about you

- Overly posed pictures, formal pictures or those taken as part of a professional photo shoot may be the norm in places like America, but in the UK they usually stand out as being way over the top. People may think your picture is a fake or that you are desperate to cover up your everyday looks.

- A picture showing you enjoying one of your hobbies can be a good way of showing people what you are about. Avoid blatantly posed photos as they are generally tacky and pretentious. This is especially true if the activity depicted in the picture is not one you usually participate in. There's no need to try and impress people by pretending to be something you're not. Your best bet is to choose natural-looking photos where you are doing something you regularly enjoy.

- A picture taken next to a yacht, car, etc. can make you appear overly materialistic and will usually deter rather than attract others. This is also one sure way of attracting gold-diggers. Pictures of you standing next to hobby-related vehicles such as a sailboat or a motorbike could possibly be an exception to this rule, although could still make you look like you're trying too hard to impress.

- A picture of you on a good night out says you are a fun person who knows how to have a good time. A picture where you are obviously drunk, under the influence or hungover, however, will make people think you are an alcoholic or worse.

- A blurry, soft-focus, or poor quality photo will make people think you have something to hide. Is it wrinkles? Horns? Your face, so your wife won't find out you're dating? Most people would pass you by if you uploaded something like that.

- A picture where you are pulling a face may well show people your silly side, but is not likely to be at all flattering. Even people who appreciate a good laugh may be put off by someone who can't keep a straight face for the time it takes to snap a single photo.

■ A picture where you look sultry and aloof is likely to make you look unpleasant and pretentious more than anything else. Copying expressions from film stars, pop stars, etc. is not going to help you on a dating site. The image celebrities usually go for is unattainable beauty. Their faces are saying: 'I'm too good for you and you will never have me.' If you are trying to get people to approach you, you don't want to look unattainable, you need to look approachable: smile!

Chapter 5

Finding the right people

In this chapter you will find out about:

■ The different types of search methods

■ Strategies for search

■ How to read profiles critically

Different search types

There are two types of search method available on dating sites. These are active search systems and passive search systems. They both have their advantages and disadvantages.

Active search system

Most sites are based on the *active search* system. You select a number of criteria, run the search and a list of people is generated. Active searching gives you a lot of control, because you are the one determining the exact qualities you are looking for in a person. This method is popular because most of us have a pretty good idea of what we're after and want to start looking at potential dates as soon as possible. Barring any technical problems, active searching will deliver you a list of potential matches almost instantly. The qualities you can use to define your search will depend on what the site you are using offers as searchable data. Most commonly, they will include basic information such as age, location, marital status, build, etc. Some sites allow you to search by other factors such as interests, profession, level of income, level of education and so on.

Advantages

If you get tired of searching for a particular type of person, you can easily change your criteria in your next search and start again. Some sites will also allow you to save your searches and run them again at a later date, in case more people fitting your criteria have joined in the meantime. It's up to you to keep searching for new people whenever you feel you have exhausted your options. When you do that, you may find that your search results keep coming up with people whom you have already seen.

Disadvantages

There are a few downsides to active searching. The fact that the search criteria provided by most sites are superficial at best will often result in long lists containing many unsuitable matches. You can easily see what I mean by trying a simple experiment next time you are walking down a busy street. Let's say you are attracted to tall men with blonde hair and blue eyes. Take a look around you and see how many of the people around you fall under that description. How many of those do you actually fancy? Out of those, how many do you think would also be compatible with you? Probably not very many, unless you are extremely lucky or not very fussy.

Running a simple search on a big dating site can sometimes result in hundreds of potential matches. Statistically, it's highly unlikely that you would be attracted to every single one of those people.

Passive searching

The second generation of dating sites includes some sites with a different search mechanism referred to as *passive searching*. On such sites, members don't run searches themselves, but let the sites' matching software select and present people to them. This is generally done based on more detailed personal information that is provided by each user at the registration stage. It could come in the form of a personality test, psychological compatibility test, astrological map, numerological name analysis and just about anything you, I, and online dating entrepreneurs can think of. Some of these things are pretty gimmicky, but they have come about as an attempt to go deeper into the 'science' of compatibility and find different ways of matching people up. Do they work? Well, that depends on your definition. Thousands of people meet and fall in love on such websites every day and have happy, long-lasting relationships, so obviously these sites do work. Then again, thousands of people fall in love on other dating sites too, where the search method is based simply on ticking a few boxes and then looking at people's pictures.

Are you compatible?
The concept behind passive search sites is not a million miles away from the concept that drives things like arranged marriages: the belief that immediate attraction is not necessarily the basis of a good, long-lasting relationship. People who support this theory believe that you should put your trust in more 'relevant' factors if you are to find true compatibility. What you would define as relevant would depend on your own belief system: you may think someone's astrological chart has a direct bearing on whether you two would make a good couple, or you may think having compatible personality types is more important. Whatever you believe, it's good to keep in mind that even the best site with the most impressive-sounding matching software can only take you so far. When dealing with human beings and things like attraction and love, there is never a definitive answer.

Luckily, unlike arranged marriages, dating sites using the passive model only take us some of the way. They present us with a list of people they deem as suitable for our needs and leave us to make a selection based on our more 'superficial' criteria (such as whether or not we fancy the person).

Disadvantages

Passive searching often takes longer, as the site will continuously offer you more matches as new members sign up. How often you get new matches will depend on the site's settings and the number of members who fit the bill. If the site you are on doesn't have enough members it deems suitable for you, you may be waiting a while.

Sites that rely solely on passive searching usually charge more for membership, saying they are giving you a better service by offering use of their scientific matching system. For this reason, as well as anything else, you should do some background reading about the site you are considering and make sure you are happy with the sound of the system used. If you join a site that only offers passive searching, you will depend on that matching system to bring people to you. You need to be able to trust this system not only to find matches that are right for you, but also not to wrongfully reject suitable matches.

I once saw a site that claimed to match people based on a personality test. When I came to take the 'test', it turned out there was only one question. The question went: 'Are you an introvert or an extrovert?' There was a short explanation of the meaning of each option, but nothing more. Once you ticked the box, the site started searching for your matches. Somehow I don't think that site was particularly scientific. Any couples who met on there would have done so because of sheer luck. If you are going to rely on luck, you may as well save a few pounds and use one of the many sites that let you actively run searches yourself.

Active and *passive searching*

The most important thing to keep in mind is the fact that passive search systems are designed to only look at particular factors of compatibility. They are never to be seen as the be all and end all of the dating world. Just the fact that a site has deemed you incompatible with someone doesn't mean you couldn't be compatible in many other ways. In fact, sites that offer both active and passive searching are fast replacing exclusive passive search-based sites for exactly this reason.

Less is more, more is less

When we meet people in real life, we usually end up dating people who are not 100% like our ideal partner. While secretly we may be hoping to one day marry Johnny Depp or Cameron Diaz, we often bend the rules and fall in love with other people too. More often than not, when we look back on our choice of past partners we find that they had some qualities we didn't like. Had we been able to design the perfect partner, he would have perhaps been a little thinner, a bit richer, and maybe slightly less grumpy in the morning. Yet here we were, quite happily dating people who weren't technically our ideal match. Would those people have made the cut online? On dating sites, you can only contact people through a filter: either your search criteria or the site's own assessment of you and your requirements. Anyone who doesn't fit the bill, anyone who doesn't look good on paper, will be kept away. You will simply not see him.

Knowing what's important

If you want to keep your options reasonably open, you will need to have a think about the makings of your ideal partner and see what qualities you would be willing to compromise on for the right person.

Obviously, some things are more important than others. You may want someone who shares your religious beliefs or political outlook, for example, and refuse to even look at anyone who doesn't comply with these requirements. Other things, such as eye colour, profession, etc., may be a bit less important to you, but really important to someone else. When designing your search, it's worth remembering that the more detailed your search criteria are, the more limiting they would be. You may want someone who is 25-35 years of age, but what if he was perfect for you in every other way but was actually 24 or 36? You may specify that you prefer someone who is a non-smoker, but what if you met someone who was otherwise perfect but smoked?

The answers to these are entirely individual and you should be honest with yourself about what you would and wouldn't agree to settle for before making your choices.

There is no harm in starting your search by looking for your perfect man or woman. However, if you find that you are not getting as many results as you might like (which will probably be the case if you have a very specific set of requirements), expand your criteria slowly, making adjustments as you go along.

Start with the things that matter the least and keep expanding until you've reached the realm of your deal breakers: there is no reason to search for people you are not likely to ever want to date.

Timescale for searching

You should expect a site to deliver you at least some potentially suitable profiles on your first active search attempt; two or three is not an unreasonable number. By potentially suitable, I mean those who match your criteria and look attractive enough in their picture for you to believe you could date them.

Be wary of sites that offer you no matches at all when running an active search. They probably don't have a big enough membership in your area to match your requirements.

Unless you live in a very small, faraway place, most big sites should deliver you at least a few new results if you run a search about once a week. If you live in a big city like London and run a generic age/sex/location search, you should expect any big site to deliver you several new results even if you run a search once a day.

If you do live somewhere remote, your choices may be limited and you will probably want to join several sites and run regular searches on all of them (or expand your search to include people who are further away). A shortage of frequent results in this case, especially in response to a very specific search, is not necessarily an indication that the site is bad.

Passive search sites often take a few days to deliver results. The better ones will specify the average waiting time. If you have limited your search radius to a small and remote area, you may wish to expand it and see how well you do then. A site that fails to deliver you any matches at all within a week is most likely not suitable for your needs.

A note about long-distance relationships

The Internet is a great place, because it allows us to meet people from all over the world. As a result, we are often faced with the question of long-distance relationships.

Many people choose to limit their search criteria to their immediate area to avoid dealing with this issue, but occasionally people who live far apart do come across each other online. Distance is just one factor in the relationship equation. Like any other factor, its level of importance is a matter of individual opinion. Is it worth getting to know someone who lives far away? Would a long-distance relationship be a recipe for disappointment or could it be a very wonderful thing?

It's worth thinking about the following questions before you start your search.

- Would you be up for meeting someone from another part of the country?
- How about a different country altogether?

Long-distance relationships are difficult and demand a certain amount of sacrifice from the very beginning. Keeping a relationship going when you are apart for most of the time is not easy and relocation is often difficult and sometimes even impossible. However, long-distance relationships are not impossible. I personally know a large number of people who met over the Internet and travelled across half the world to be together. Some of these people are now living together quite happily and some are even married with children. Unfortunately, not all such relationships end well: I also know many people who followed the dream only to discover it had no basis in reality.

Once you make a connection with someone, it's often impossible to give up the dream without giving it a go, no matter how far apart you are and how crazy it may seem. Such adventurousness can be very exciting, but also rather costly at times. The only way to protect yourself from having to make such decisions would be to make sure you never even see people who live outside your area. Many sites nowadays offer UK-only dating, which can help.

If you are open to dating people from further away, or if you are finding that the choice of interesting people in your area is limited, consider expanding your search to people from other areas. If you then do find someone, listen to your heart but make sure you know the risks and complications involved before you go down that route.

Reading profiles critically

Remember all the things I told you to never put in your profile? This is when it will all make sense. When you're scanning a list of profiles for people to talk to, you simply don't have the time to psychoanalyse every single person and consider whether or not any mitigating circumstances exist. If something looks fishy, you will run like the wind – and who can blame you? I am not going to encourage you to look beyond the text and give people a chance if you find something strange or unappealing. This may sound harsh, but I do believe there are a lot of people out there who are not ready to date again but are doing so anyway. Getting involved with anyone like that is a recipe for disaster. Luckily, in most cases warning signs will exist that can warn you off such people until they have got over their issues.

The bad signs

Here are a few of those bad signs:

- People who say they are looking for 'discreet, no-strings fun' are usually married and looking for an affair. There are more tips on how to spot these 'lovely' individuals in Chapter 9.

- Talking about past heartbreak in the profile, frequent mentions of an ex and derogatory comments about the opposite sex all point to baggage and unresolved issues.

- Beware of profiles that look too good to be true as they are often made up by scammers who are out to steal your money (more about this in Chapter 2 and Chapter 9).

- If a person's profile states that he is interested in a casual relationship or activity partners only, believe him. Unless this is what you want as well, you would be setting yourself up for failure if you contact someone like that. This is one case where the warning is definitely on the label.

■ Watch out for anyone who goes on at length about physical characteristics without mentioning anything else. Also beware of anyone who states in his profile that he has a web camera and looking to have some 'adult fun', 'camera fun', 'adult chat', etc. These are the telltale signs of someone who's only interested in sex or cybersex.

Giving people a chance

While some people translate well into the online world, others don't. People who don't spend a lot of time in front of computers, for example, may not be as comfortable expressing themselves in writing as those who do it for a living. Sometimes people will let you know they are uncomfortable with this form of self-expression, but other times you will be left to figure all this out on your own. Making allowances for people on the assumption that they may be more eloquent in real life can therefore sometimes pay off. After all, it's not a virtual relationship you're after but an actual one.

Photos can also only go so far. Obviously, physical attraction is a factor that is more important to some people than to others. You may have a strong opinion of the physical type you are attracted to, or you may not. I am not here to tell you that looks shouldn't matter, because they obviously do to many people. Unless you are setting out to find a platonic relationship, you will want to find someone you are attracted to. It's up to you to decide what constitutes that attraction and what factors you're willing to compromise on. There is absolutely no shame in wanting to be with someone who appeals to you physically. Both you and your chosen partner deserve to be in a relationship where mutual attraction exists. I'm not saying only 'pretty' people deserve to find love, but rather that physical/sexual chemistry is an important factor in most relationships. You should know your own feelings about being able to develop such attraction based on non-physical qualities and be willing to act on them as you see fit.

Of course, the fact that a person appears attractive or unattractive in a photo or video does not necessarily mean the same would be true in real life. You will probably know if someone has no chance of ever appealing to you without resorting to plastic surgery, but there are some cases when it's more of a grey area. Two pictures of the same person can appear completely different: which one is a true likeness? To complicate matters even more, some people are simply not photogenic. Charisma, for example, that elusive quality that endows seemingly unattractive people with magnetism, is notoriously hard to see in pictures. Because of this, it's sometimes worth contacting people you think you *may* be attracted to on the basis of their personality. You'll never know for sure whether you have chemistry until you meet in person.

Chapter 6

The first move

In this chapter you will find out about:

■ Communicating non-verbally online

■ The makings of a good first message

■ Responding to people

■ Dealing with rejection

Should I contact people or wait for them to contact me?

If you've gone to the trouble of setting up a profile and paying your membership fee, you'll want to get your money's worth. You could sit back and wait for the right person to find you and contact you, or you could do something about it yourself, which is far more effective. Remember that by placing your profile on a dating site you're already saying you want to meet people for the purposes of dating. Any attempt at coyness under such circumstances would be pointless to say the least. If you are uncomfortable with the prospect of openly admitting to yourself and others that you are looking for someone, standard online dating may not be for you. Take a look at Chapter 12 for alternative ways of meeting people on the Internet.

There is often a misconception among women that they have to sit back and wait for men to contact them unless they want to be seen as too forward. Whatever you do, don't fall for this sort of dated nonsense. Even traditional dating has mostly moved away from this notion, with most men nowadays being flattered and responsive when a woman approaches them. This is certainly the case online, where things are generally much flirtier: it's perfectly acceptable for both men and women to make the first move.

Another excuse I've heard for not wanting to contact people is that letting someone know you are interested may give him the upper hand in a relationship. This is based on the deluded theory that states women must treat men like crap in order to make them interested. Unfortunately, there is also a theory that states men need to treat women like crap in order to gain *their* interest. If everyone played along with these rules, the whole world would look like one of those awkward school discos where the boys and girls occupy opposite sides of the room and are all too shy to speak to each other. It would definitely make for a very poor online dating experience for all of us.

The fact of the matter is, whether you are a man or a woman, sitting back and waiting for prince or princess charming to contact you can be a long, boring process, during which you may be spending a lot of money on membership and getting very little in return. If you like the look of someone, let him know. Even if you prefer not to send the first message, there are some subtle ways you can do it that don't involve sending an actual message. I will be discussing these shortly.

Women get more messages

Sorry boys, it seems that women have more luck when it comes to being able to sit back and enjoy the ride. Women generally seem to get more attention than men online, but rest assured it's not always welcome attention. I am not sure why things are the way they are. It could be because there are more male than female daters, it could be that men are generally less fussy or it could be because some women are still wary of making the first move. Who knows? Either way, the fact of the matter is that men still have to work harder to get noticed online.

How many people should I contact?

Some of your success in the world of online dating will depend on sheer luck. Unless you are extremely lucky from the start, your dating will predominantly be a numbers game. The way to think about it is this:

■ Not everyone you contact will write back

■ Not everyone who writes back will be worth meeting

■ Not everyone you meet will be worth meeting again

■ Not everyone you start dating will turn out to be a long-term partner

The more people you contact, the more chance you have of finding the right person. It's as simple as that.

In the online dating world, both men and women are more or less expected to keep their options open for a while, at least until they meet their chosen dates in person. There is no point in limiting your options at this early stage by pinning all your hopes on one person. Have a look around and contact anyone you think may be worth getting to know.

Sending a signal

Coming up with something original to write as a first message is not always easy. On some sites, you can bypass the need to think up something witty by using any number of clever features that allow you to send a subtle signal without actually saying anything. These features are usually free even on pay sites, which mean many people will use them as a way of gauging the level of response before deciding whether or not to pay.

Profile viewing

The first of these signals is a very subtle one, which was most likely not designed as a means of communication, but has taken on a life of its own on some sites. This is the feature that lets you see who viewed your profile and how often. People who want to be contacted but don't want to make the first move will sometimes view a person's profile repeatedly, thus hinting that they are interested. Because of its subtlety, this feature is not always so effective. Its success depends on the other person knowing it exists and using it in order to check his profile views. Obviously, if you are going to use something like this, you will need a very well crafted profile with a really flattering picture to match. After all, it's those features you'd be relying on to get you a response to your efforts.

Icebreakers

One step up from this, are the features known as icebreakers: 'kisses', 'flirts', 'winks' etc. These are little set messages you can send someone at the push of a button. Their appearance differs from site to site. Sometimes all the contactee will get is a message saying he got a 'kiss', with a link to sender's profile and possibly a picture. On other sites, you may be able to choose from a list of pre-written messages to send.

This is a quick, non-committal way to let a person know you are interested. It's very simple to run a search and then spend ten minutes sending each person on the list a 'kiss' or a 'flirt'. You could easily contact dozens or even hundreds of people like that without much effort and without paying any money. That's the good news. The bad news is that each person in question would know that you had chosen this way of contacting him rather than taking the time to compose a personal message. As a result, a lot of people may decide you're not worth replying to. Don't expect to get the same level of response as you would if you had written to each one individually. However, you may still get some favourable responses. If people see your profile and like what they see, there is no reason why they shouldn't reply. Again, this is another time when having a good profile would work in your favour.

Multi-user messaging

On some sites, you can compose your own message and send it to a large number of people at once. While still not as good as a personal message, being able to write something yourself means you can write the message in a way that will make it seem personally targeted. Most sites won't let the members on the other end know that they have received a mass mail-out, so you can safely pretend it wasn't one. I've come across quite a few people who started their mass messages by apologising for the generic message and asking to be contacted anyway. In my experience, this is a very big mistake. Most people won't bother responding to a message that wasn't sent personally to them.

Bad mass messages
Imagine opening your mailbox to find a message like this:

> Hey boys!
> Sorry about the mass mail-out but I'm afraid I don't have time to message all of you individually. Why not take a look at my profile, and if you like what you see, give me a buzz and we can have a chat.

Or this:

> Any girls out there up for some fun with a guy like me? Give me a shout if you do.

Not exactly the sort of thing that makes one feel special, is it? Plus you already know you are competing with lots of other men or women for attention.

Good mass messages
You would probably be more inclined to reply if someone you find attractive sent you a message like this:

> Hi there,
> I liked your profile, I think you look really cool. There's so much more I'd like to know though! Take a look at my profile, if you like what you see, then maybe you can message me back and we can have a chat sometime?

Or this:

> Hi there,
> My name is John, but you can probably tell that from my profile. I was
> looking around and came across your profile and thought, 'Hey, she
> looks nice!' so I thought I'd say hi and see if you'd like to have a chat
> sometime. Give me a shout if you like what you see.

There's absolutely no reason why a message like that couldn't light the spark
that would result in a long-term relationship, or even marriage. In fact,
during my role as customer advisor, I got quite a few 'thank you' notes from
people who met on our sites as a result of messages just like these.

If someone gets your message, replies to you and you start talking, the fact
that your original message was sent to a few more people will not matter. If
you feel the need to apologise, you can do it during the message conversation you have as a result.

In all cases, avoid including caveats, exclusions etc. in your message like in
the example below:

> I want to meet a woman in my area, but I am not interested in anyone
> over 5'10'. If you are over 5'10' please don't contact me.

Apart from betraying the fact that this is an impersonal message, this sort of
thing (especially when applied to weight, race, etc.) can offend many people,
including those you are trying to appeal to in the first place.

Replying to signals

Because profile views, icebreakers and multi-user messages are impersonal by
nature, you shouldn't feel obliged to act on any of them if you don't want to.

Profile views

If your site offers you the chance to see who viewed your profile, do it. It's
entertaining, if nothing else. If someone you fancy has viewed your profile
repeatedly, it's up to you whether you want to start a conversation.

Icebreakers

The same goes for icebreakers: people who send these won't get offended if you don't reply (and if they really want an answer, they can send you a real message). The nature of icebreakers is that you will undoubtedly get a large number of them, usually from people fishing for responses before deciding on whether to subscribe. Replying to each and every one of those would be a waste of your time and energy.

Multi-user messages

As for multi-user messages, you don't have to reply to them either but sometimes you may not know them for what they are.

As a rule, any message that lands in your mailbox from someone you may be interested in is worth replying to, regardless of its nature. You owe it to yourself to chase every possible lead. Don't be offended, though, if it turns out to have been a multi-user message and the sender is not really interested. These things can sometimes happen.

The only time you are expected to reply is if you sent a multi-user message yourself and have received a message back. Remember: the other person thinks you contacted him directly and are interested in him. It's only polite to say something, even if it is an explanation and a polite rejection.

Here is an example of what you could say if you are not interested:

> Hi there,
>
> I'm really sorry, but the message I sent was actually a <insert name of mass-messaging feature here> that got to you by mistake.
>
> I apologise if I gave you the wrong impression, but I don't actually think we'd be very compatible.
>
> Good luck in your search!

The first message

As you can probably guess from the proliferation of first-message alternatives, a lot of online daters are a bit wary of making the first move. Sending the first message needn't be an awkward chore, though. All you are doing is making someone know you exist and inviting him to check you out and send a message back if interested. With personal messages, you are in complete control of the text and have the added benefit of being able to tailor each message to its intended recipient.

So what's the problem with sending the first message? I believe a lot of it boils down to fear of rejection. So before we move on to discuss the workings and makings of a good first message, let's take some time out and get this issue out of the way.

Let there be no doubt in your mind: sometimes you will send a message and not get anything back. There are many reasons why a person may not answer your message:

- He is no longer an active member on the site
- He is already communicating with someone (or several people) and is not looking to meet anyone else for now
- He gets loads of messages and never has the chance to read (or reply to) all of them
- He feels you would be incompatible for a particular reason
- He does not find you attractive
- Something you said in your profile may have put him off
- Any number of other personal reasons

Most of these reasons would have nothing to do with you whatsoever and they are far more common than you might think. Most of us, though, feel rejected when we don't get a response. Our insecurities rise up and make us assume the worst. The important thing is to keep trying and not take these non-rejections to heart. A certain amount of dead ends is absolutely normal and you'd be doing yourself a massive service by accepting this and not letting it bother you or stop you from contacting people.

Your objectives

More often than not, the people you send your first messages to will see the message before they see your profile. Your message should, therefore, conform to similar guidelines as the ones referring to your profile and picture.

When making first contact you have three objectives:

- Making the receiver of the message know you exist
- Making that person want to get to know you better
- Starting a conversation

Similarly to the profile, the first message should be positive and upbeat. There is no room for sob stories here either.

Things that should go into a first message

A brief introduction with a little bit of information about you
There is no point repeating all the information already available in your profile. Give a few highlights instead, or write something you haven't put in the profile already. If the message does its job, the recipient will go and read your profile anyway.

The reason why you chose to contact this particular person
This is your key to making your messages individual and appealing. When you explain to someone why you have contacted him, stay away from personal reasons ('I'm bored and looking for a chat', 'I need a date for Valentine's Day'). Instead, really read the person's profile (even if you're only really interested in the picture) and comment on the things you find there. You want to let the person know why you have chosen to contact him rather than any of the other people out there.

Both men and women like to be made to feel special. In this case, you can make anyone feel special by showing him you have taken the time to read his profile and liked what you saw. It's perfectly acceptable to compliment someone on his appearance, as long as you keep your message polite and non-sexual. If you liked someone's smile, for example, say it. It may seem trite but everyone loves getting compliments. Although originality does help, you don't have to compare anyone's eyes to the raging sea on a winter's night to get a good response.

If you share interests, hobbies, likes and dislikes with someone, mention this and talk about them. This is one of those times when you can get away with writing a longer message, as it would likely be one the other person will want to read.

A hook (or several) to keep the conversation going

A conversation is an exchange of information between two people. This may go without saying, but sometimes people are so eager to let others know they exist, they forget to include anything in their message that would give someone the opportunity to easily respond. What you need are handy *hooks* to make it easy for the other person to reply to your message. These hooks can either be a call-to-action or some leading questions. A call-to-action is an advertising term used to describe phrases such as 'call now' and 'visit your local store today'. They are meant to encourage the reader to do something in response to seeing the advert.

Here are a few examples of call-to-actions you can use:

> Message me back and tell me about your trip to the Congo, it sounds fascinating!
>
> Send me a chat request if you're around. I promise I'll reply!
>
> Take a look at my profile and let me know what you think.

Leading questions are an even better way of getting people to reply. Pick up on things in their profile or picture and ask for more information. Alternatively, point them at your own profile and ask them what they think about something. Beware of asking too many questions and making your message seem like an interrogation, as that may put people off.

Here are a few examples of good questions to ask:

> Is that your cat in the picture? It looks so cute! Is it a male or a female cat? What's its name?
>
> I noticed you've been to India too. I just got back from there a few weeks ago. Which parts did you go to?
>
> Check out my picture section if you want a laugh! I dyed my hair green on a dare. Do you think I should keep it like this?

As usual, these are rough guidelines rather than a formula you should follow. Dating sites would be pretty boring places if everyone sent each other the same messages all the time.

Style

Brevity

Generally, opening messages are kept relatively short, to simulate the beginning of a conversation. A length of about a paragraph or two will usually be enough; there is no need to write whole essays here. I've seen too many people write lengthy messages telling their life story with hardly any reference to the recipient's profile. Most people wouldn't bother reading past the first couple of paragraphs when presented with something like that. On the other hand, if you find someone who seems interesting and you think you may have a lot in common, writing a longer message that goes beyond the usual 'Hi there, check out my profile' can actually work in your favour. Remember that in the online universe, a long, involved message means you are excited and interested. When two people find each other on a dating site and realise they share many common interests or traits, that is certainly cause for excitement.

Informality

Messages may be written, but that doesn't mean they have to read like formal letters. Nowadays, most people have some idea of online communications, but for some, these involve mostly business emails. Where I work, we keep business emails fairly casual, occasionally ignoring greetings, formalities and even punctuation. In other places, business emails are written in much the same way as standard business letters. Whatever the case may be with your online writing experience, messages on online dating sites are fairly casual things. Remember, though, that you are introducing yourself to someone for the first time so including a greeting and some information about yourself is therefore a good idea.

Humour

Feel free to use humour in your messages. If you can make someone laugh, you'll probably get a message back. If you want to know what's funny, think about what makes you laugh. There is no point trying to guess someone else's sense of humour, unless you are trying to gauge whether or not he would be offended by something.

Tone

Remember that tone and non-verbal communications are completely lost online. If you are writing something that could be read in several different ways, there is no guarantee it will be read the correct way by others. The online universe has developed its own ways of dealing with this, in the shape of emoticons (i.e. smileys etc.) denoting various emotions, as well as annoying abbreviations such as 'lol' (laugh out loud) that tell people you are joking. I am as guilty as anyone of resorting to smiley faces whenever I use dry or sarcastic humour online. In my experience, though, people who are new to the Internet don't always get the point, which has been known to get me in trouble occasionally. As a rule, it's best to simplify the language you are using, rather than rely on symbols that may be as obscure as the tone you'd intended.

Things to avoid when contacting people for the first time

Disrespecting people's wishes

If a woman states in her profile that she only wants to be contacted by blonde men and you are a redhead – don't contact her. If a man says he doesn't want to hear from women with kids and you have kids – leave him alone. Blatantly ignoring people's wishes like that will not get you anywhere. In most cases, there is nothing you can say or do that would change people's minds, so why contact them in the first place? Always read the person's profile before sending a message, to see if he's got any exclusions on there that you should be aware of.

Now, I realise that sometimes it's possible to be completely blown away by someone's profile and think that you are perfect for each other. You may then decide to throw caution to the wind, hoping things will work out between you anyway. In all honesty, they usually don't. People who go to the trouble of putting exclusions in their profiles know what they want and, more importantly, what they don't want. Still, if you are convinced you've found the person for you, who am I to stop you from trying to contact him? If you must do it, be honest; apologise for contacting the person against his wishes (which is exactly what you would be doing) and explain why you think it could work out between you anyway. Don't expect a reply and don't be offended if you don't get one. It won't hurt to even say in your message that you will understand if you don't get a response – it would make the message seem less intrusive. If you fail to win the person over, give up and move on.

Leery or cheeky comments, asking for sex and anything that could be seen as too forward
Unless someone's profile says he is looking for sex, keep it clean. The only places where it's perfectly acceptable to comment on someone's physical attributes and ask for a shag straight away are the sex sites. Try it anywhere else and you will get nowhere; even some innuendos may be too much for some people. You can usually tell from reading someone's profile whether that person would be comfortable with a certain level of cheekiness, but in case of doubt, don't risk it. Once you've got to know someone a bit, it will all become clear.

Asking for too much too soon
As a rule, asking to meet up in person in the first message is generally considered inappropriate. Even those daters who want to keep online contact to a minimum will want to know a bit more about someone before deciding whether a date is a good idea. There are no short cuts. Giving a lot of personal information in your first message won't help speed up the process.

Giving an email address/phone number etc. and asking people to contact you directly
Apart from the obvious safety risk to you (see Chapter 8 for more information), this sort of thing would make you look cheap. Most people choose to be on dating sites because they can keep their details safe from people they don't know yet. They would need a good reason to abandon this safety and speak to someone off-site. Wanting to save a stranger a few pounds is not usually considered a good reason.

If you tell people you can only be contacted off-site, most of them won't bother getting in touch at all. If you have signed up for a free or short trial period, you can let people know your time is limited, but try not to make it sound like you are pressuring them into replying just to save yourself some cash.

Self-deprecation and making apologies

Just like your profile, your first message should give people reasons to contact you, as opposed to reasons *not* to contact you. You don't have to apologise for things people can judge for themselves. If you dislike expressing yourself in writing and want to make people know there is more to you than meets the eye, you can use the message to explain this. Otherwise, keep it positive and let people make their own minds up.

Boasting

As already discussed in Chapter 3, boasting won't win you many admirers. A single boasting sentence can sometimes seem harmless enough as part of a balanced profile, but could make you look positively arrogant if it were part of a three-sentence message.

When you are turned down

Sometimes when you send a message to someone, that person may reply and say he is not interested.

Unless the message is offensive in itself, there is no need to be offended by this: different people have different tastes. In some cases, it could be a matter of timing and nothing more. Most people send such messages out of kindness, to prevent others from building their hopes up or assuming the worst. Never enter into a conversation with such a person, even if you only want to thank him for letting you know. It isn't expected of you and most people would view such a message as a nuisance or an attempt on your behalf to change their mind.

If the reply *is* offensive, you can treat the user as a problem user and take appropriate measures (discussed further in Chapter 9).

Replying to unwanted messages

In an ideal world we would only get contacted by people we fancied. In an almost ideal world, we would get a few unwanted messages and would politely reply, saying 'thanks, but no thanks'. The person being thus rejected would accept our verdict gracefully and never bother us again. We'd all live happily ever after.

In reality, we may not have time to reply to every single person who's written to us and we may prefer to only reply to people we may actually want to date. We may feel awkward about writing to people in order to reject them and feel it may be best to just ignore them and hope they go away. When we do write to someone to let him know we are not interested, we may find that the person in question is not very graceful about the situation at all.

Remember that just because someone sent you a message, doesn't mean you have to reply. Just because you are not interested in someone, doesn't mean you owe anyone an explanation or an apology. It may be a nice idea to reply to everyone who contacted you and let them off gently, but most people wouldn't expect you to and (hopefully) you would be too busy replying to people you actually *want* to talk to.

How you behave in situations like these is therefore entirely up to you. Treating people as you would like to be treated is generally a good rule of thumb. You will soon find out, however, that behaving in a certain way is no guarantee that you will receive the same treatment from others. The majority of people are selective about which unwanted messages they reply to, although some people reply to every message they get. Others choose to ignore anyone who isn't of immediate interest to them. Any of these are acceptable.

If you are going to send a message back, be polite but firm. You don't want to give the impression that you *may* be interested. There is no need to explain *why* you don't think it would work ('You are too fat', 'You are too skinny', 'I want someone with more money') but no need to be overly diplomatic either. Saying something like 'You never know, but I think it probably won't work between us' could make someone think he may be in with a chance. Be clear and leave no room for doubt. If the person in question doesn't get the hint, don't enter into a conversation with him. If you get any more messages (even if they are only saying something like 'thanks for letting me know, good luck') ignore them. This is where the conversation should end, as there is nothing more for either of you to say to each other.

If the person keeps messaging you, it may be time to treat him as a problem user and react accordingly (see Chapter 9 for more information).

Chapter 7

Online interaction and beyond

In this chapter you will find out about:

- How long to spend communicating online

- The different means of online interaction

- Learning about people online

Getting to know each other

Once you've made initial contact and received a response, you can start getting to know the other person better. A common way of progressing along the communications path is to begin by exchanging standard messages, move on to real-time chat (instant messaging) if available and then move on to speaking on the phone. Obviously, there are many variations on this theme with some people opting to leave out various stages as they see fit.

Your objectives

Your main goal from now on is to find out if the person you are talking to is likely to turn out to be someone you could end up dating. When communicating with someone online you therefore want to:

- Find out as much as possible about the person you are talking to
- Give information about yourself in return

When speaking to someone, you will want to find out whether you both see eye to eye about the issues that matter to you, but you will also want to know whether you click. After all, having the same deal breakers does not in itself guarantee a relationship or even initial attraction.

Pacing yourself

I once spoke to a man about his failed attempt at online dating. He'd recently moved to London to work in the IT industry and didn't know many people in town. Being an active person in his early 30s, he wanted to spend his leisure time away from his computer, enjoying the many cultural attractions on offer. He generally felt a lot more comfortable talking to people in person than online. 'I was hoping I could sign up to a dating site, find people I wanted to get to know and then arrange dates pretty quickly', he told me. To his dismay, he discovered that the women he met on the site wanted to speak online for a while before going on a date, which he saw as a sign they weren't really interested in meeting. He became frustrated and bored and decided the whole thing was a waste of time.

Another time, a woman I know complained to me about her own experience of online dating. 'All the men just want to meet up straight away', she said. 'Surely if they wanted anything more than sex, they would take the time to get to know me first?' She had also decided online dating was full of time-wasters.

When I talk to people about online dating, these are among the most common complaints I hear. It seems that there are two different schools of online dating that have opposing views on what the medium is for and how to use it effectively. Just like in traditional dating, some daters like to move fast while others prefer a gentler pace. Some daters begin their online dating experience by rushing through the online stage and going on as many dates as possible. They eventually slow down as they learn to read profiles more critically. For others, the process is reversed with initial mistrust turning into confidence and a more outgoing attitude.

When someone from the 'Take your time' school meets someone from the 'get on with it' school, things can get a bit bumpy to say the least. As in the examples above, people often misinterpret each other's motives and assume the worst. When you look at it objectively, though, there are plenty of reasons why people may find either one of these methods appealing.

Reasons why people may want to take their time

- They have been hurt before and are being cautious

- They are shy or express themselves better in writing

- They are insecure about their looks

- They have little free time and only want to go on dates with suitable people

- They are easing themselves into the dating game and are enjoying the online social life

- They have children and are wary of letting strangers into their lives without vetting them first

Reasons why people want to take things off-site quicker

- They express themselves better in person or on the phone

- They work with computers and don't want to spend their free time online as well

- They are busy or active people and want to spend their free time socialising in the real world

- They see the online dating experience as a means of introduction only

- They don't believe you can really tell what a person is like online

I believe the best use of online dating involves finding the happy medium between the two above extremes. How fast you wish to take things will depend entirely on your lifestyle, personal preferences and circumstances.

Whatever you decide, you are likely to find that people's demands and expectations vary greatly even on the same dating site, although some sites will attract a particular type of crowd. Younger, flirtier sites, for example, will likely be faster-paced environments, while those sites aimed at facilitating serious relationships will appeal to more cautious daters.

How many people should I talk to?

As discussed in the previous chapter, it's good to keep your options open when dating online. Messaging is a casual thing, a bit like speaking to a few people at a party or a speed-dating event. No one would expect you to keep things exclusive at such an early stage (if someone does, take it as a sign that he is a bit too clingy). Whether you are a man or a woman, I encourage you to message as many people as you want. Apart from being a means to an end, dating is a fun activity in itself. Meeting new people, knowing that you have options and simply socialising and flirting with others are all great confidence boosters. Feel free to enjoy these regardless of your age, gender or circumstances.

The different means of interaction

Messaging

These are basically like emails, but exchanged on the site. Much like the first message, the following messages can be a combination of information about you as well as something to make it easy for the other person to reply. There is no need to follow a formula here. Remember that you are having a conversation with someone, so it's better to let it flow naturally than to try to stick to any rigid rules.

Language styles

People use different styles when it comes to the language they use online. Really there are no conventions. In general, most people tend to use plain English in their messages and not 'textspeak' (i.e. 'gr8' instead of 'great', etc.) but some do stray. While it helps to be aware of the meaning of these abbreviations, you shouldn't feel obliged to use them unless you particularly want to. For a list of common abbreviations, see the Appendix 2 at the end of this book.

Composing messages

When sending standard messages you can take your time and compose your replies carefully, which can be rather convenient. Of course, the other person can also do exactly the same thing and so, if you are trying to figure out what someone is like, getting your information from standard messages or emails could give you a less-than-accurate picture.

Checking messages

While some people log in to a site every day to check their messages, others don't. If you've sent someone a message and he didn't reply, there is no point sending another message again on the same day. Wait a few days (three or four) and if you've still heard nothing back, you can send a short message to check whether your first one was received. If you don't get a reply to your second message, it may be time to give up.

Length of message

When having a message conversation with someone you've recently made contact with, keep your messages relatively short (a few paragraphs on average). Avoid replying to short messages by writing really long ones unless the occasion really calls for it. Unsolicited long messages can be rather overwhelming: it's essentially the online equivalent of bursting into a long monologue on a first date when the other person has hardly said anything. As the conversation progresses, you will likely send both long and short messages to each other, similar to the natural flow of a conversation.

Honesty

Be honest and don't be afraid to talk about how you're feeling. If you are finding the situation strange or amusing or if you are worried about asking personal questions, say so. If you think something you are saying can be read in more than one way, explain it. It's easy to misinterpret things online, where we don't have the benefit of body language and tone to help us understand. Honesty and clarity are the best methods of getting things across. Even a bit of over-explanation is better than giving someone the wrong impression by accident.

Keeping conversations going

Hopefully by this point you will have enough material to talk about, as a result of your first message exchange. Like real-life conversations, though, online exchanges have their own ebbs and flows. If the person you are talking to is a bit of a 'closer' (i.e. someone who answers your questions in full but doesn't ask any in return) you'll need to keep coming up with more questions to ask or topics to talk about, if you want to keep the conversation going. Limit these to a few at a time so that your messages don't look like a quiz. You can also ask the person whether he wants to know anything about you.

Endings

Unlike an instant messaging session, that has a definite, natural end (such as when one of the people has to go and do something else), you could theo-retically carry on a standard messaging session forever. As a result, there don't seem to be any conventions regarding the polite way to end this kind of exchange. Be prepared to have conversations fizzle off into nothingness or stop at unexpected points. In the majority of cases, such incidents have no hidden meaning and the conversation can carry on as normal at a later date or start again with a different topic.

Try something new

Be willing to move to (or at least try) instant messaging sooner rather than later. It may not be your cup of tea (in which case, you can either return to messaging, or call each other on the phone) but it's worth a go, as it's a real-time exchange and closer in structure to a normal conversation.

Instant messaging

Sites vary in the type of instant messaging (chat) they offer their users. The most common type is a basic, text-only chat. Fancier chats offer the chance to use a microphone or a web camera (if you have them) to enhance the experience.

Instant messaging is not entirely unlike trying to write a transcript of a conversation while it's happening. It's also not entirely dissimilar to text message (SMS) conversations.

If you're not used to chatting online, you may find the experience a bit strange at first, but once you get used to it you will be able to translate your thoughts into a flow of written text without too much effort. The key is to write like you would talk, without letting the fact that you are typing fool you into thinking you have to be official or literary.

Because chatting resembles a normal conversation in its flow, I see it as a better way of figuring someone out online. Many people find this anonymous form of chatting quite liberating and end up having quite meaningful conversations with complete strangers, which can be quite a lot of fun.

You can say no

Just because someone asks you for a chat, doesn't mean you are expected to accept. This is particularly true in cases when you are asked to participate in camera/video chat by random strangers. Men asking women for this are notorious for wanting to have cybersex, rather than actually chat. Feel free to reject any request that looks suspicious or ask for clarification about the nature of the chat by standard message before accepting. In general, people who ask for 'camera fun' and similar terms are all after the same thing. It almost goes without saying that this sort of behaviour is not acceptable on all but the most blatantly sexual sites. While cybersex/net sex does happen online (and on dating sites) between people who are into it, it's by no means an integral part of the experience. Anyone who tries to convince you it's a requirement is either grossly mistaken or a liar.

Abbreviations

Because instant messaging requires faster typing, people generally tend to use more abbreviations and smileys. This is a matter of convenience, rather than something that is expected of everyone.

Off-site chat

If your site does not offer instant messaging, you may decide to make use of one of the various free chat platforms such as MSN Messenger, Yahoo Messenger, ICQ etc. Even if your site offers instant messaging, you may still want to chat off-site at some point, as it may be more convenient. If you do, it's worth spending a bit more time messaging on the site first, to find out more about the person you are talking to.

Most Windows PCs will have a version of MSN Messenger on them that you can use. If you don't already have an account, you will need to set one up, which you can do when you load up the program for the first time. If your Messenger ID is your usual email address, you may want to set up a different one to use when you are speaking to people you don't know very well.

Speaking on the phone
After an hour or so of chatting to someone online (either continuously or over a few sessions) you should be able to have a pretty good idea of whether you would like to speak to the person on the phone.

Phone conversations

Depending on your personal circumstances, you may be more or less keen on speaking to people you've met through a dating site. Most of us nowadays have mobile phones and I suggest you use a mobile phone to speak to your new online friends, rather than your home phone. It's quite common for people to buy a cheap pay-as-you-go SIM card and use a different number for all their Internet-related calls. Some people also use Skype, which is a bit of software that allows you to route phone calls over the Internet (it has the added benefit of being free). These methods allow you to extend your anonymity to the next stage of communications, as you may like to hear the sound of someone's voice before deciding whether or not to give him access to your real phone number.

Awkwardness
In the same way that some people have problems expressing themselves in writing, others feel uncomfortable speaking on the phone. Even people who are very confident and charming in person can sometimes sound awkward and nervous and send the entirely wrong signal. Sometimes it's hard to tell whether an awkward phone conversation is just that, or a sign that you are incompatible. It may be worth meeting up in person so that you can tell for sure.

A stranger's voice

If you have been chatting online for a while and have spoken about personal issues, the transition to a phone conversation can be a bit strange. This is because the brain gets mixed signals under such circumstances: the voice is the voice of a stranger, but there is certain familiarity there already. This is one of the main reasons why it's best to move to phone conversations pretty early on, although the weird feeling usually passes after a short while.

Learning about people online

There is only so much you can learn about a person by speaking to him online, but it is still possible to learn quite a bit – definitely enough to know whether it's worth taking things further. Sadly, there is no way of telling in advance whether you will be physically attracted to someone. Some things can only be determined when you meet up in person.

Posing questions

Although online dating allows the possibility of getting deal breakers out of the way early, there is a curious discrepancy when it comes to asking those same questions as part of a conversation (be it standard messaging, instant messaging or phone calls). Most people would feel awkward when asked a direct question about topics such as level of income and whether or not they want children, unless that question was asked as part of their standard registration process.

If you know what your deal breakers are and feel strongly about them, I suggest you choose a site that incorporates this sort of information into a less intimidating feature such as search criteria or the sign up process. If you have to ask, build up to the serious questions as you would in a normal conversation by asking a few less personal ones. With it being online dating, you will probably end up talking about such serious issues sooner, rather than later, but allowing the conversation to flow naturally will help make things seem less threatening.

The telltale signs

You can tell a lot about a person's state of mind by the way he speaks about his job, his leisure activities and his last major break-up. This is by no means a foolproof way of gauging someone's complete personality, but it can certainly highlight a few important aspects of it.

When people think or care about something a great deal, they usually tend to talk about it a lot. When you ask someone about the three items above, start by paying attention to the amount of time he spends talking about each one. A person who has a lot to say about his work but less so about his activities outside of work is likely to be mostly work-oriented. Sometimes people have a particularly good or bad day at work and so might talk about work quite a lot, when usually they wouldn't so much. If you are trying to gauge how important somebody's job is to him, pay attention to whether what he's talking about is a particular incident at work or the merits of the job itself. As always, if this is an important issue for you, ask a direct question.

As a rule, if a person mentions his ex frequently in a conversation about anything apart from his last relationship, that is an indication that his ex is still very much at the front of his mind: the more frequent the mentions, the stronger the association. Beware of anyone who goes into a long speech or rant about a bad break-up. He may not be ready to date again. Some people even go as far as renouncing all members of their opposite sex, which should be an even stronger indication that you should stay away.

The way a person chooses to spend his leisure time can be a good indication of whether you two are compatible. It's good to speak about what a person would like to do, as well as what he does at the moment to get the complete picture.

If someone has little to say about his job or dismisses it as being 'boring' and then has little to say about his leisure activities as well, it could mean that person is generally dissatisfied with his life or even depressed. Unfortunately, it's quite common for all of us to sometimes concentrate on what we'd like to change in our lives rather than what makes us happy. However, the amount of time someone spends talking about the bad aspects vs the good aspects of his life can show you whether this is a positive or negative person.

Dealing with dead ends

If you have exchanged a few messages with someone or chatted to him, it's only fair to let him down gently if, for whatever reason, you have decided to stop speaking to him. Unfortunately, not everybody does that.

Even when you think things are going well, some people may still end up doing a disappearing act. Sometimes this won't be such a big deal, in which case you can just let it go and assume that the person you've been speaking to is no longer interested, for whatever reason. If you don't want to give up without a struggle, you can try sending another message to see if you can get a response. There are some people out there who believe in playing games and making people jump through hoops, so you may get somewhere if you persist. Remember, though, that there is a fine line between persistence and nagging. If someone disappears without an explanation, wait a week and send your second message. If you get nothing, you should probably give up. There is no point trying to guess what could have made the person stop talking to you. More often than not it wouldn't be anything to do with you at all. The best thing you can do is let it go and find someone better to speak to.

Sometimes sites do have technical problems and if you've been having a great conversation with someone who's disappeared, you may be tempted to think your messages are not being received. If you really think this is the case, you can email the site's support team and ask them to tell you if there are any problems. Be aware, though, that online dating sites and their staff are bound by privacy laws – the same laws that protect you from having your personal information revealed to others. Telling you whether a particular person has received a message you sent could be seen as a violation of the site's privacy policy. Luckily, asking whether your messages are being sent out *in general* or whether the site is experiencing any technical glitches should get you some sort of answer. The bad news is that more often than not a technical glitch is not the problem.

Treat any rejection as final, even if you get the 'it's not you, it's me' line or anything that may imply things may change in the future. Sometimes people say that just to be nice and, either way, life's too short to wait around for anyone.

Letting people down gently

Let's face it, saying to someone that you don't want to speak to him anymore can be awkward – not something any of us ever look forward to. As a responsible writer, it's my duty to encourage you to take the time to write to people you don't want to speak to anymore, but ultimately how you act is up to you. If you have been exchanging messages or chatting, people will expect a reply and would be surprised if you ignore them. You can either:

a. Ignore them anyway

b. Tell the truth and say you don't think you are compatible (using the 'let's be friends' line, as appropriate)

c. Tell a white lie

Unless you are interested in staying friends, this is where the conversation should end. Never continue communicating in order to justify your reasons. No means no. If a person you turned down persists and is annoying or offensive, you can treat him as a problem user and refer to Chapter 9 for advice on how to act.

Chapter 8

Online safety rules at a glance

In this chapter you will find out about:

■ Online dating dangers

■ The basics of keeping safe

Exercise caution

The majority of online daters have a perfectly hassle-free experience, far from the scare-tales you may have heard or read. Unfortunately, this does not mean the online dating scene is entirely free of dodgy people. There are all kinds of undesirables online that you will need to watch out for.

Obviously, it is my job to prepare you for anything I can think of that may threaten you online. For the purposes of this chapter, the next chapter and the safety section of Chapter 10, we'll have to tackle some worst-case scenarios. When presented together and taken out of context, these could make you think online dating is a pretty dangerous place. Don't panic: online dating is only dangerous in the same way traditional dating is dangerous. It's perfectly safe, as long as you keep your wits about you, use your common sense and follow some basic safety rules.

> **Remember:** The people you meet online are strangers. Obviously, not all strangers are bad, but until you have established that the person you are talking to is OK, you will need to exercise caution.

The dangers

The bad people who lurk online can be divided into three loose categories:

- Dangerous people (murderers, rapists, paedophiles, etc.)
- People who are after your money (scammers, prostitutes, etc.)
- Harmless but annoying people (offensive users or 'cyberstalkers').

You may have heard stories about women being killed by men they met online. The chances of you coming across a murderer or a rapist are extremely, extremely unlikely. In fact, it's the rarity of such cases that makes them newsworthy in the first place. Can you imagine a newspaper headline saying, 'thirty million women *didn't* get murdered by men they met online today'? Scammers are very common, but also the easiest to spot and avoid. In all likelihood, the most severe problem you'll ever come across will involve having to deal with someone from the third category, i.e. an offensive user.

Am I being paranoid?

Some of the safety rules in this chapter may seem a bit extreme, especially once you've been on a few dates with perfectly normal, non-murderous people. In fact, some might say these rules are a bit paranoid. At the end of the day, you can use your own sense of better judgement to decide how far you want to go with these rules. Just remember that while we all say 'it will never happen to me', sometimes 'it' does happen to people who didn't expect it to.

Keeping your information personal

Your personal details such as your full name, postal address, phone number(s) and email address are all precious assets. You shouldn't dish them out to any random person without stopping to consider the implications. A dating site acts like a buffer zone between you and the strangers you are talking to. You can find out whether you are compatible with someone without having to divulge any of your personal details. This is a very good thing, so don't throw it away by plastering your details all over your profile. Saving a few pounds is not worth compromising your personal safety.

Addresses

Unless you have a PO Box that is different from both your home and work address, don't share your postal address with anyone until you are convinced he is not likely to be a psycho. Ideally, you shouldn't do this until you've met this person face-to-face at least once.

Even seemingly meaningless information can be enough for someone to be able to find out where you live, work or hang out, so be careful what information you give out. If you live and work in a small town or work for a well-known company, it may be easy for someone to find your office address if you give out the company name. There is nothing freakier than someone turning up at your workplace to surprise you, having figured out the location from random things you said.

Phone numbers

Your home phone number can be used to find your address, which is why it's best to give out a mobile number instead. If you need to call someone from your home number and want to be safe, block your caller ID.

Full names

Your full name can be used to track you down, especially if you live in a small town or have an unusual name. If you are on the edited version of the electoral roll a determined person could look you up using your real name and any information he has about your general location. There are now some websites out there that allow people to do this very easily. If you are one of those people who have a big online presence, giving someone your full name would also allow him to 'Google' you and find anything the Internet has to say about you. This could be stuff like your place of work, where you study etc. depending on what's out there.

Email address

Unless it contains your full name, your email address is generally pretty safe to give out, as long as it isn'ts your work address that has your company name as the domain name. Remember, though, that most cases of harassment and stalking that happen as a result of online dating involve online harassment, rather than actual stalking. Once a problem user has your email address, things can get rather irksome. Online harassment could mean bombarding you with pathetic/offensive emails but also more sinister events such as sending you dodgy things to get you in trouble at work. For this reason, it's best to create a free email account and use that to communicate with the people you meet online, at least until you know they're OK to talk to.

Safety Dos and Don'ts

These are the online equivalent of locking your door, hiding your valuables and not walking through bad neighbourhoods alone at night.

- If at all possible, try to keep all of your online communications confined to the dating site you're on. If someone is giving you grief on the site, the moderators will be able to check the history and find the offensive messages. They will then be able to remove the user if necessary. Moderators can't act based on exchanges that happen outside of their jurisdiction, i.e. emails, phone calls, off-site chat sessions, etc.

- Save all emails and log your chats when communicating with people off-site. This won't be of use when you want to get someone's account removed on a dating site, but can come in handy in more serious cases of harassment etc. (and if the person is just fine and you end up falling in love, you'll have something to remind you of how you met).

- Watch out for things that are too good to be true and things that are out of place. Users from a foreign country on a site that is advertised as UK-only must have done something dodgy to get on there in the first place. Men and women who look like runway models and say they make more than £100k a year are more likely to be scammers than your prince or princess charming.

- Beware of anyone who asks you a lot of personal questions without providing any information about himself in return. If someone avoids simple questions he may have something to hide.

- Beware of anyone who gives inconsistent answers to your questions, makes any angry or offensive remarks (even if he apologises later) or disappears for long periods without an explanation. Any of these could be a sign that something is not as it should be.

- Avoid anyone who tries to get you to communicate off-site straight away. Scammers often do this to save money and avoid the long arm of the moderators.

- Beware of anyone who is jealous and possessive towards you before you even meet. If someone sounds angry or overly upset about the prospect of you speaking to other people, going out with your friends instead of speaking to him online etc., treat it as a warning sign and stay away.

- While there is no harm in asking someone out on a date early on, coercing or pressuring anyone into speeding up the dating process is wrong. If someone is disrespectful of your boundaries in this way, he will likely be disrespectful of your boundaries in real life as well. Avoid this type of person.

- Trust your instincts. If you are getting a bad vibe off someone you are speaking to online, there is probably a reason for it. Don't make excuses or let it go thinking you are being silly or overreacting. If you have a history of going out with abusive people, be extra careful and make sure you take the time to find out some information about each person you speak to. You could also get a friend to look at the person's profile and give you a second opinion.

- If you are a parent, beware of anyone who seems to show an excessive interest in your children. It's important to point out at this point that I don't think a few harmless questions about kids are a sign that someone is a paedophile. After all, it's only polite to show interest, plus, if the other person you are speaking to is also a single parent, this could be an obvious topic of conversation. Actual paedophiles are not as common as you might think and in 99.9% of the time this will be a non-issue. However, if you come across someone who makes you uneasy by constantly asking questions about stuff like your children's daily routines, the location of their school, etc. trust your instincts and stay away.

■ Never share your login details with anyone else. This could seem a harmless enough thing to do, but giving someone access to your profile means that person can then pretend to be you and do any number of bad things in your name. If you use a public computer to log in to a dating site, make sure you log out properly, rather than just closing the browser. You should delete the cookies at the end of your session after you have logged out. (If you use Windows Explorer you can do this by going to the 'tools' menu, selecting 'Internet options' and then clicking on 'delete cookies'.) This will prevent the next person using the computer from being able to log into your account automatically. Make sure you never save your password on a shared computer. If you find a nice profile on the site and want to show your friends, test the link you send them and ensure that it is not the kind that would automatically log them into your account when they click on it.

■ This is probably the most important one of them all:

Never send money to anyone you've only spoken to online or on the phone no matter what sob story they tell you.

People who ask for money are usually scammers and you will read more about them in the next chapter.

A note about moderation

Many people who use the Internet fall under the illusion that what they say and do on the Net is entirely private. In fact, most things you do online, unless encrypted, can technically be read by others. If you use any of the free messaging services without encrypting your message, your service provider could technically read any of your messages. This is not usually done, because of the sheer volume of messages that pass through the service every day.

All messages on dating sites are kept somewhere on a server. Yes, these are the messages that users send each other privately on the site. The people who moderate the sites don't usually read these, but they are still easily accessible to them if required. Depending on the moderation policy of the site, the moderators would most likely only look at profiles and pictures: things that are readily and publicly available on the site. Private messages are only ever read in cases when there are complaints about a particular user. Site owners are also required by law to hand copies of such messages to the police if requested. This is one of the things that makes online dating safe, as everything you say and do on there is logged. If someone hassles you on the site, you would be able to easily obtain proof if needed.

You may not like the fact that your personal messages can be read by others on the site. Before I became a moderator, I used to cringe at the thought of someone having access to my personal messages. I imagined all moderators to be nosey, intrusive people who enjoyed reading other people's stuff. Once I became one, though, and spent many long hours reading message board posts, profiles, blogs etc. for a living, I quickly learned that the last thing any moderator wants to do is read any messages when he doesn't absolutely have to. In fact, professional moderators don't really read: they scan large volumes of texts for particular words or phrases, without taking in any irrelevant information. Rather than worry about this issue, you can relax knowing that you can use it to your advantage if you find yourself being harassed by anyone online.

Chapter 9

Problem users and how to deal with them

In this chapter you will find out more about:

■ Scammers

■ Liars and cheats

■ Offensive users

■ Stalkers and bullies

Scammers

Scammers are extremely common in the online dating world. Luckily, the majority of them are sloppy and very easy to spot when you know what to look for. In fact, once you know the telltale signs, you may well wonder how anyone could possibly fall for such transparent ploys. Unfortunately, scammers are never short of victims.

Scammers are only after one thing: money. Because of this, they often favour sites that are free or cheap to use. Sites that are 100% free to use are often infested with them. Sadly, even paid sites are not immune, as scammers often sign up with fake credit card details. If you spend enough time online, you will come across such profiles sooner or later.

In the industry, we loosely divide scammers into three separate groups. The common names for these are, unfortunately, not politically correct. The first group is commonly referred to as 'Russian Brides', even though the scammers in question are not always Russian in origin. The second group is known as the 'Nigerian' or 'African' scammers (because the first of these scams originated in Nigeria and then spread to other countries in Africa) and the third group includes prostitutes and premium rate phone number scams.

As some scams become old, scammers come up with new ones. You may well come across totally different scams than the ones listed here. The most important thing to remember is that all scammers want money. Sooner or later they will start asking for it, using whatever excuse or tall tale they can come up with. This is the most important sign of them all and the first one you should be looking out for.

Russian Brides

The scam
This scam has a few variations on the theme:

■ A woman (generally an attractive one) makes contact with someone via the site and at some point down the line asks for money either to help get her out of trouble or to fund her ticket to visit the man. In reality, the 'woman' may not be a woman at all (although there are genuine female scammers out there) and has no intention of ever meeting the victim. Once the money is sent, 'she' disappears, never to be heard from again.

- Similar to the above, but the woman continuously asks for more and more money. Sometimes, the woman will actually convince the victim to fly over and meet her. She will then get as much money out of him as possible. Some of these women are effectively prostitutes who sleep with the men they meet on dating sites and then ask for money.

The signs

The majority of scammers use photos of beautiful models that are obviously posed or scanned from magazines. The profiles themselves are often easy to spot as they are poorly written and paint a picture that is just a little bit *too* perfect. Recently though, some scammers have been improving their methods, writing more realistic profiles and using more down-to-earth pictures.

Without wanting to do any honest Eastern European women an injustice, I would say that any profile that boasts a model-like picture (i.e. an attractive person in an obviously posed photograph) whose owner says she is from Russia or another Eastern European country, should immediately make you suspicious. If the site you are dating on is advertised as being UK-only, you should obviously be doubly suspicious.

Russian Bride profiles are written in broken English and the grammatical errors are not always consistent with each other. They often describe themselves by using a long list of adjectives obviously taken from a thesaurus. They talk about how loving and caring they are and tend to have hobbies that are designed to make them seem especially appealing to a certain type of man (i.e. those who want a submissive woman). Scammers usually say they are looking for serious relationships, 'true love' etc. thus making their victims think they're onto a winner.

It's important to point out that not all of these scammers are Russian or even Eastern European. Dodgy profiles that follow this formula can have pictures of women from all over the world. Some scammers even register with a UK address.

Here are a couple of examples of such profiles:

I am a beautiful, attractive, pleasant, caring and gentle woman. I have been hurt in the past but now my heart is open for your love again. My hobbies are taking pictures with my camera, taking walking on beach and cooking and cleaning for my partner.

Description:
Caring, intelligent, independent, free spirited, attractive, vivacious, charming.

Looking for friendship first but then maybe love, who knows. Looking for man, appearance not important.

In their messages, Russian Brides are overly affectionate from the word go, referring to their intended victim as 'darling', 'sweetheart' etc. They quickly break into stories of woes meant to make the victim feel sorry for them.

Most scammers will try and get their victims off the site as soon as possible by providing their email address straight away, sometimes even a phone number. Don't make the mistake of assuming that someone is not a scammer because you have spoken to him or her on the phone, or even met in person. If the person then goes on to ask for money, be suspicious. Why are you the only person who can help?

What to do

- **Don't give them your money, no matter what they say!** Once you send the money, you will never get it back.

- Scammers always try to cover a lot of ground very quickly so they generally message a lot of people at the same time. If you suspect someone of being a scammer, contact the site's support team and ask for their opinion. They will have access to that user's message history and will be able to tell whether the person has been acting in a suspicious manner. People who moderate dating sites for a living have a lot of experience of spotting scammers; listening to their advice is generally a very good idea.

Nigerian or African scammers

The scam

This is exactly the same scam you may have already had sent to you in the form of email spam. These scams are usually quite ridiculous and very easy to spot on a dating site. They often involve stories intended to make you give up your bank details or use your bank account to launder money in some way. You may be told you were entered into a foreign lottery automatically and won, or that a businessman needs your help in order to help him transfer some money between accounts. Obviously, there is no such large sum of money and the 'businessmen' who contact people on the Net are nothing but scammers who want your bank details in order to rob you. I've even seen clever scams where a good 'Christian' woman asked for help in delivering money to a poor sick boy somewhere in Africa. The good woman would send a cheque, which you would put into your account and then transfer part of the money elsewhere, keeping a percentage as your 'fee'. Unfortunately, foreign cheques can be bounced for up to six months after being put into a UK bank account. A victim of such a scam would soon find himself in a very messy situation with his bank.

Nigerian and African scammers are not limited to these '411' scammers (411 is the section in Nigerian law that deals with such scams). There are some African scammers who use a similar formula to the Russian Brides scam. Unlike the Russian Brides, the African scammers target both men and women and it is not unusual to see pictures of suited, attractive men who describe themselves as loving, caring, god-fearing etc. 'God-fearing' seems to be a favoured term among scammers, who use it to fool people into thinking they are honest.

The signs
Some of these scammers actually cut and paste the entire sob story into their profiles. Others have profiles that are not too unlike the Russian Brides profiles, but will bombard you with their stupid ploys in messages.

These scammers also generally try to move you away from the site as soon as possible.

What to do
Don't give them your money. These are always scammers. There are never any real businessmen or any amount of money you could possibly get. Avoid them and report them to the moderators of the site. While some of these scams could only cost you money, others are perpetrated by violent gangs of criminals. Never be tempted to meet with such people under any circumstances.

Prostitues and premium rates

These are not as common as the other types of scammers but they do exist. They usually target men who want a quick one-night stand or phone sex and are too desperate to check their facts first.

The scam

A beautiful woman invites men to contact her as she is interested in sex or 'sexy chat' on the phone. When contact is made offline, it turns out these services are not free. These can range from a premium rate phone sex line to all out prostitution.

The signs

Similarly to the Russian Brides, these sex-workers use obviously posed pictures, often of women in bikinis or underwear. Unlike the Brides, these women usually talk about wanting 'adult fun' and being 'up for anything'. Sometimes they put phone numbers and SMS shortcodes on their profile and invite men to call or text them. Occasionally, they will include a link to a website for a 'camera chat' which will then turn out to be a porn site.

What to do

Avoid these people or report them to the moderators of the site. They can check them out and let you know if there is any foul play involved.

Liars and cheats

The problem

People (both men and women) who are married or attached and are using the Internet as a place to meet people to have an affair with. Unlike some people who are honest about their marital status and intentions, these problem users lie about their situation and pretend to be single.

The signs

- Cheaters don't want to be found out, which means they usually won't upload a photo or choose one that is blurry or otherwise unclear.

- Cheaters' profiles sometimes hint at their situation by saying they are interested in meeting people who are 'discreet' for 'no strings fun', 'casual sex' etc. If someone mentions the word 'discreet' on his profile, you should immediately start to suspect something is not quite right.

- Not all cheaters say they are interested in a casual relationship. Some will try to fool unsuspecting daters into thinking they want something more. Such cheaters can be difficult to spot straight away. When you've just made contact with someone online, it's reasonable to protect your privacy and so you shouldn't take someone's reluctance to divulge too many personal details as a sign that he is married or attached. Many people, especially single parents, want to really get to know someone before giving out any details that could potentially put their children at risk. However, if you have been seeing someone for a while and the relationship has developed, it's fair to expect that person to trust you with information like his landline number and address.

- Cheaters will not give out their home number even when you have been communicating for a while, have met and maybe even slept together.

- Cheaters won't invite you to their house or introduce you to their family and friends. They will keep coming up with new excuses and reasons why it can't happen.

- Cheaters are away and out of touch often, sometimes disappearing at short notice without giving a good explanation. They often give inconsistent answers to questions or refuse to answer them altogether.

It is said that a woman always knows. I believe any one of us, man or woman, has the ability to sense whether something isn't as it should be. The problem is that whenever emotions are concerned, we often don't want to know and ignore all the signs and signals that are clear as day in hindsight. If you end up seeing someone who is lying about their marital status, chances are you will have some sort of inkling that something is going on. Unless you have a history of severe paranoia, you should trust your instincts rather than ignore them.

Many of the signs listed above can have perfectly reasonable explanations that do not involve cheating, but a few of these things combined could mean you're onto a cheater. Keep your eyes and ears open.

What to do

Regardless of the moral implications of adultery or infidelity neither of these things is actually illegal. If you've been the victim of one of these cheaters, you will probably want his profile removed from the site to prevent other people from being similarly hurt. This may or may not be possible, depending on the policy of the dating site in question. While some dating sites uphold a 'singles only' policy, others do not. The best thing you can do is report the user, deal with your pain and hope for the best. There are now some websites out there that act as cheaters' directories where men and women post warnings about people who have hurt them, although the legal implications of doing something like that are yet to be determined.

Offensive users

The problem: harassment

Someone is being offensive or is harassing you on the site. This could be anything from swearing or using offensive language to making racist comments, etc.

What to do

Most sites will have a 'block' function that will allow you to stop a person from contacting you again. In the majority of cases, doing this will be enough to stop any further trouble. If you can't find the block function, contact the site's support team for advice. As different people have different ideas of what constitutes offensive language, the site support/moderating team will not usually take any action against users who merely used a swear word. If the matter is more serious (such as homophobia or racism) they may remove the user's account altogether.

The problem: dangerous harassment

Someone is being particularly offensive, has posted an offensive profile or has given you a reason to think he may be dangerous.

What to do

Apart from the block function, most sites will also allow you to report offensive users so that their account can be removed. If you are worried someone may be dangerous or offensive to others, contact the site's support team and explain the problem. Moderators get hundreds of messages a day from people who have fallen out. They would usually tell you to block the user, unless it looks like he is generally offensive or potentially criminal and/or dangerous.

If you come across a person you feel may be *really* dangerous you should definitely let the moderators know. Moderators have access to all the messages users send and receive so they would be able to see the bigger picture and deal with the offensive user if necessary.

Whatever you do, don't get into long, involved arguments with anyone who has offended you. Simply block him and move on. Be especially careful of fighting fire with fire, i.e. being rude and offensive back. If you need to get the support of the site's moderators afterwards, being offensive yourself is not likely to work in your favour.

Stalkers and bullies

Unfortunately, these particular nasties are far from uncommon online, although they seem to frequent some sites more than others. For the purposes of this book, the stalkers/bullies can be divided into two categories: those who confine their activity to cyberspace and those whose antisocial behaviour extends to real life.

Be aware that while the majority of stalking is done by men towards women, there are plenty of women out there who stalk and harass men. Female stalkers can be just as annoying and dangerous as their male counterparts and yet men are far less likely than women to take appropriate measures to protect themselves from women. I am not sure whether it's male pride that stands in the way, flattery, or sympathy towards the female stalker, but really they are all equally invalid. Whether you are a man or a woman, if you are being stalked, your first priority should be your own safety. Never underestimate the situation: even the most harmless incident can turn nasty. There has been much research conducted into the personality profiles of online stalkers and bullies, but unless you are auditioning for sainthood, you shouldn't overly concern yourself with the reasons behind their actions. All you need to know is that what we're dealing with here are people with serious mental health problems. If you come across them, don't worry about their feelings; worry about your personal safety and take appropriate measures.

Cyberstalkers and bullies on your dating site

One of the reasons online dating used to get such a bad rap is the fact that it's very easy to engage in antisocial behaviour online. In fact, many people who are quiet and reserved in real life use the Internet as an outlet for their frustration and anger. The irony is, though, that the online dating medium is actually a very good defence against random stalkers. Unless you are careless and choose to flaunt your personal details on your profile, no one who finds your picture online will be able to find your phone number or physical address. This instantly gives you more control over situations which you would normally be unable to prevent.

The problem
A cyberstalker may come across your picture on a dating site and decide you are the perfect partner for him, refusing to accept anything you say as proof that he is wrong. Sometimes, such stalkers turn nasty when denied and start being rude and offensive.

What to do
Block, block and block again! Just like when dealing with any other offensive user, this is your best option. Never enter into discussions with a cyberstalker. If you feel that a rejection is needed, be polite but firm. Avoid using any phrases that can make the stalker think you may ever change your mind. Doing that would be far worse for both of you than making it clear you will never be interested. Once you have given your rejection, block the user.

If you are getting offensive messages, don't lower yourself to that level. Send a message back saying something along the lines of 'please stop contacting me' and then simply ignore the messages and block the user. Stalkers and bullies are like little children throwing a tantrum: pay no attention to them and they will get bored and go away.

Be aware, though, that depending on the way a site is set up, a stalker may still be able to rejoin the site using a different name. If you have already told this person to stop contacting you, there is no reason to do so again. Ignore the messages, block the new username as well and keep reporting him to the site's owners. Sooner or later he will get bored and go away.

Cyberstalkers and bullies who contact you off-site

The problem
You have shared your email address, MSN, Yahoo! or AOL messenger IDs, etc. with someone who is now stalking you.

The signs
If you have started messaging someone online and are wondering whether or not to give out your email address or Messenger ID, watch out for the following, as they can be signs that you are dealing with a potential stalker:

- Someone who is being very possessive and jealous, expecting you to stop speaking to other people on the site and wanting to know your whereabouts all the time

- Someone who is overly affectionate and/or declares his love to you before you have even met

- Someone who tries to guilt trip or bully you into giving out personal details before you are ready

- Someone who sends you lots of unsolicited messages a day (as in, messages that are not a part of a mutual exchange)

What to do
If someone is stalking you online but not on the dating site, you should:

- Keep all emails sent to you and any chat logs involving conversations between you and your stalker. You can set up just about any chat client to log conversations automatically. If possible, copy these logs/emails to a floppy disk or CD so that you have a backup in case something happens to your computer. This is important evidence.

- Contact the stalker's online service provider with your evidence and ask for the user to be dealt with. This can be done by emailing the address abuse@provider where 'provider' should be replaced by the stalker's own Internet Service Provider (such as gmail.com, hotmail.com, etc.). Don't do this before you ensure that the domain name a stalker is emailing from is indeed the ISP's domain name (like hotmail, gmail, BT, etc.) and not one the stalker owns himself. If you can't tell, email your own service provider's support team and ask for their advice. Remember that a stalker can open another Internet account even when removed from one ISP, but there is nothing stopping you from getting him removed again and again until he gets the point and stops hassling you.

■ If you or your ISP operate a spam filter, you can use it to block the stalker's email address, although doing this will prevent you from collecting further evidence if needed. Only do this when you're sure the person could never find your whereabouts or is harmless.

■ If your stalker exhibits threatening behaviour, collect your evidence and contact the police. The Protection from Harassment Act is your friend and covers situations like these.

■ Never underestimate this kind of stalking. A determined stalker can find out everything he needs to know from details such as your full name. This is much easier than you can imagine.

When stalking goes further

While it's easier to deal with stalkers on the Internet, things can be more troublesome when they extend beyond the virtual. Many instances of stalking don't begin until a relationship ends. By that point, you could have been seeing someone for a while and have shared with him more valuable details such as your phone number and address.

The problem

Offline stalking can include sending things through the post, making nuisance or malicious phone calls or following people around. In extreme cases it can involve violent acts. Offline stalking as a result of online dating is usually the result of a relationship that starts online and ends either immediately after meeting in person or shortly afterwards.

The signs

As well as the signs already discussed above, alarm bells should be going off if you are in a relationship with a person who behaves in any of the following ways:

■ Wants to know where you are all the time, calls you frequently to check and acts in a possessive/jealous manner

■ Disapproves of you spending time with your friends and family

- Bullies or coerces you into doing what he wants, even when you don't want to do it

- Constantly demands attention and reacts badly when denied

- Declares love very early in the relationship and expects you to do the same

- Is clingy and doesn't respect your space

- Is often angry

- Is abusive to you, your friends or family members

- Makes threats of violence or is actually violent

- Wants the relationship to advance faster than you do and is not respectful of your own feelings on the matter

- Spies on you or follows you around

- Sends you unwelcome presents

What to do

- Make it clear to the stalker that you are not interested in any further contact with him and that your feelings will never change. Be firm. It's better to be assertive than be overly polite and give the wrong impression. Stalkers will try to make you feel guilty so you let them down gently and then use your pity and sympathy as proof that you really love them. In a stalker's mind, anything apart from a firm 'no' can be turned into hope for the future. 'I want to be single right now' means 'I will change my mind later' to a stalker. 'I think maybe we shouldn't see each other' would make a stalker think you have doubts. Don't fall into the trap.

- Once you have made your feelings absolutely clear, sever all contact with the stalker. If you receive letters or gifts in the post, do not reply, send them back or destroy them. Keep them as evidence but avoid reacting to them in any way. If the stalker phones you, do not speak to him. Leave the phone off the hook for a while so that it costs him money and then hang up. You can report malicious phone calls to BT or any other service provider. Keep records of the time and length of each call and the caller ID if possible. The police and your service provider can get the caller ID even if the stalker blocks it, so don't worry if you can't get it yourself. If you can, tape the calls and keep any messages. It's best to use an answerphone for this, rather than a voicemail service, so that you can keep the tape.

- If the stalker approaches you on the street, refuse to talk to him. Ask him to leave you alone and walk away. Don't be afraid of making a public scene if you feel you are in danger.

- Keep a diary and make a note of everything that happens, including any suspicious activity and any contact with the stalker.

- Tell everyone you know that you are being stalked. This will prevent your stalker from getting information about you via other people. There is no shame in being stalked, even if you are a man being stalked by a woman. It's better to swallow your pride and be safe than to have the stalker cause you problems.

- Always carry your mobile phone with you. If you are a woman, get a rape alarm as well. If you think you are being followed, go to a public area and call the police. It may be a good idea to check out your local area and note any places that are likely to be open and busy at all times, so that you know where to go in case of trouble.

- While you are being stalked, avoid going places on your own at night. If you live alone, you may want to invite someone to stay or go and stay somewhere else.

- Vary your daily routine to make it difficult for the stalker to figure out where you're going to be at any given point. Tell people at work you are being stalked to pre-empt any trouble your stalker may attempt to cause you.

- Never agree to meet the stalker alone, even if he promises you he will stop stalking you if you do. This is exactly when the really bad things can happen.

- If you have children, inform their teachers that you are being stalked. Talk to your children and make sure they know not to speak to any strangers and to tell you if anyone tries to approach them. Try to vary your children's daily routine so that it's not easy to predict.

- Contact the police as soon as possible and ask for their advice. The Protection from Harassment Act means they can now act faster to protect you, as stalking falls under the definition of antisocial behaviour. Don't be afraid of contacting the police every time the stalker approaches you, threatens you, shows up on your doorstep, etc. Stalking can be just as much of a problem when it's a woman doing the stalking and a man being stalked. Your first priority is to remove the threat to your safety or peace of mind so that you can go back to leading a normal life.

Further reading

http://www.bullyonline.org/related/stalking.htm

An American site with general advice about bullying and stalking. This is their section about stalking and cyberstalking, with references to articles about cyberbullying as well.

www.nss.org.uk

A British charity set up to help victims of stalking.

http://www.supportline.org.uk/problems/stalking.php

Information and advice about stalking as well as a list of useful links for further reading.

http://www.oft.gov.uk/Consumer/Scams/Online+dating+scams.htm

UK Office of Fair Trading advice about online dating scams.

Chapter 10

Meeting up

In this chapter you will find out about:

■ When and where to meet

■ Safety tips

■ Dating etiquette

How soon should you meet?

The short answer is: you should meet when both you and the other person feel ready. The timescale for this will depend entirely on you. Ideally, you should meet up within a week or two of speaking to someone online, unless there are issues involved such as distance, time constraints, etc. If you speak regularly for about two weeks, you should be able to know enough about each other to be able to tell if it's worth meeting up for a date. Some people make up their minds much quicker (in a matter of days), while others need more time to decide. Only you can tell when the time is right for you to meet up with someone. Like everything else in the relationship world, this is another issue where a compromise may be necessary in order to keep everyone happy. Most people would want some information before agreeing to go on a date, but wouldn't wait around for one for longer than a few weeks without being given a very good reason.

Remember that you are here to make real relationships, not virtual ones; work towards meeting people, as this is your ultimate goal. Don't be sucked into the virtual dating world to the point where meeting up seems like a chore or a special occasion. If you want to succeed, you will have to meet up with a lot of people and accept those dates, even the bad ones, as an essential part of the process. Be ready to chase any lead that looks like it could turn into something. Be willing to follow your heart and any whims or hunches you may get: it's often the least likely ones that will surprise you.

Choose a timescale and pace to match your own lifestyle. For single social urbanites, I recommend moving a bit quicker, at least to begin with, so that you can learn how profiles relate to the people who have written them. As you learn, you will become more discerning and filter out unsuitable people without having to see them in person. For single parents or anyone else who may have reasons to be wary of letting random strangers into his life too quickly, I recommend a slower course of action. Send more messages, ask more questions and speak on the phone more before going on dates. You can gradually become more social, as you build up a level of confidence and trust. In all cases, you must never force yourself or be pressured into meeting someone before you feel ready. If you are unsure about whether or not you want to meet someone in person, wait. There may be a very good reason why you're not convinced. You could even be sensing some kind of danger signal without realising it. Never humour someone at the expense of your personal safety and peace of mind, even if it means letting that person go.

If you've been dating online for a while and have never felt ready to meet up with *anyone*, it may mean you are generally mistrustful of online dating. Otherwise, fear is there for a reason and you should follow your instincts. It's better to give up on online dating altogether than force yourself into a situation that makes you feel uncomfortable.

> *'Should I stop communicating with other users on the site once I've arranged to go on a date with someone?'*

Absolutely not! Although women often struggle with this issue more than men, some men also believe they should show a bit of 'loyalty' once they have made a connection. Keeping your options open and seeing a few people at the same time is something that is often frowned upon in the UK but is perfectly normal in other countries. Until you have gone on a date and seen whether you click with someone, there is no reason to change any of your habits. Even after the first date, it would probably be too soon to tell whether you are a perfect match. Until you know for sure, there's nothing that says you should stop searching.

A date is just a date

Technology is a funny thing. The same technology that makes it possible for us to connect with people who are far away makes it possible for us to distance ourselves from those who are nearby. In the old days when we wanted to see our friends, we would go and visit them, because phones weren't very common. When phones became a household item, going to visit someone became a more meaningful gesture to some people. Nowadays, a lot of us use text messages to contact people instead of phoning. Getting a call rather than a text could therefore now be seen as a more meaningful event.

It's the same with online dating. When we spend so much time online trying to pick the right person to meet up with, the date itself can seem like a very meaningful thing. It isn't really. A first date is just that, nothing more. It can be exciting and/or scary, but ultimately it's only a meeting between two people to see whether they click. Meeting up with someone is not a precious thing that should be saved for a special occasion and for *that* special person. It's something you should be doing frequently, if not constantly, if you are to get any sort of results. Until you meet someone in person, you will never know whether you are a match. No amount of online or phone interaction could possibly give you all the information you need. While a good first date in itself would rarely be enough to judge whether someone is your perfect match, it would allow you decide whether any potential exists. It's the best thing you can do to avoid wasting your time. There is no need to be overly dramatic about the first date. Build it up into a common part of your online dating routine and it will soon seem like a perfectly harmless experience.

Be yourself

Putting on a front to impress your date is inadvisable in the same way as it's inadvisable to lie in your profile or use a misleading picture. There is no need for it and it won't do you any favours. Make a good impression by showing *your* best side and being the best *you* can be at this moment in time.

For example, if you are the sort of person who always wears a pair of jeans and a t-shirt, there is no need to buy a suit to wear on your first date. Clean jeans and a t-shirt would do just fine. As far as behaviour is concerned, be respectful, polite and attentive, smile and try to enjoy yourself; speak about things that interest you and things you find important. This should be enough to make a good impression on anyone who is right for you.

Remember that you don't have to apologise for who you are and what you like. If it looks like you and your date are incompatible to the point where you feel compelled to pretend you're someone else, this is probably not the person for you. Rather than worry about it, put it down to experience and move on.

Reality vs fiction

One thing you will soon learn about dating online is that it's very easy to create a mental image of someone in your head that turns out to be completely false. The longer you wait before meeting up with someone, the more likely you will be to create such a mental image. What happens when you meet under such circumstances is a bit like what happens when you watch a film after reading the book it was based on. The film could be great, but you'd still be annoyed if everything weren't exactly as you'd imagined it. There is nothing you can do to stop this from happening completely. Even if you arranged to meet someone after only reading his profile (which isn't particularly advisable) you would still bring some expectations with you to the date. Reality can be disappointing, but not always. You may well be pleasantly surprised if you give the person a chance.

The perfect date

So it's time for your first date. You want the setting to be perfectly romantic so as to set the tone for a beautiful relationship, right? Actually, no, far from it. Remember that you are meeting someone for the first time. You don't know whether you fancy him, click with him or even like him. You will have learned enough from your previous communications to know that there might be something there, but until you can tell for sure, the last thing you want or need is a serious 'date' situation. This would put pressure on the both of you to act as if you are already lovers, which could look rather ill advised if your date turns out to be a freak.

This isn't to say that you should choose the local kebab shop as the scene of your first introduction, but rather that you shouldn't assume anything at this point. What you need to do is hope for the best while planning for the worst at the same time. Do put on a nice outfit if you are so inclined (it's better to be fabulous on a bad date than a slob on a hot one) but set the tone of the occasion to informal and casual, rather than strictly romantic.

The time, the place

What time of day is best for your first date? The paranoid school of online dating states that you shouldn't have your first date in the evening or at night, to prevent a situation where you feel obliged to go home with someone 'because the situation demands it'. Obviously, this is aimed more at women than at men, as it's assumed the men would be the ones trying to get the women into bed. Following this advice can sometimes be a pain, though, and really, it may not be that essential. You may well prefer to meet people after work, rather than on the weekends, especially if you are a single parent and want to spend the weekend with your kids. In regards to the situation 'demanding' anything, only you can tell whether you are the sort of person who sees this as an actual danger. In most cases, it would be a non-issue. Yes, it's good to keep in mind that you can do other things on a first date apart from go to a restaurant for dinner, but in today's world you don't have to sacrifice your schedule to keep things non-committal. There are other things you can do that would easily send the same signal to your date.

For your date, you need a place that is public enough to be safe, but is quiet enough to allow you to speak without shouting. Choose somewhere that reflects your lifestyle and the interests/preferences that you share with your date.

Some ideas for good first date places are:

- A pub or bar
- A café
- A gallery or museum
- A restaurant
- A fair, a market or a car boot sale
- A sporting activity such as roller-skating, ice-skating, rock climbing etc.
- A craft event like pottery decorating etc.
- A wine tasting, cooking class or any other hobby-related activity

The first four items on the list are all casual activities that can be either extended or cut short according to whether or not there is chemistry between you and your date. In fact, this is what makes bars, pubs and cafés the most popular location for first dates (apart from the fact that alcohol is served in pubs). Fairs, galleries, etc. are handy alternatives for people who want more interesting (or less boozy) first dates. A restaurant can potentially be the most presumptuous place to meet, especially if it's one that has a romantic atmosphere. If you and your date end up having zero chemistry, things could get rather awkward. It's best to meet at a pub or café first and move to a restaurant if things go well.

The last four items on the list are good as icebreakers but if your date turns out to be a dud you may find yourself trapped in a lengthy activity with someone you don't want to be with. They are therefore best suited for going out in group situations, such as double dates or chaperoned dates (see below) where such awkward situations can be easily diffused.

You'll note that passive activities such as films, plays, poetry readings, lectures, etc. are missing from my list. Apart from the fact that some of these include sitting in dark rooms, they also don't allow for much conversation. This makes them rather unsuitable for the purpose of getting to know someone. At best, they could be worked into a longer date, where you also do something social like go for a drink or a meal.

Safety tips for your first date

It's generally assumed and accepted that it's women who need more protection when meeting men through the Internet. However, the below safety rules can and should be followed by men as well. It's also worth pointing out that many of these rules are here to protect you not just from worst-case scenarios but also from the far more common bad-date scenarios. Taking precautions in advance will not only keep you safe but can also save you from much awkwardness and time wasting.

- Meet somewhere neutral where there are plenty of other people around. Never arrange for anyone to come and pick you up at your house or workplace and never agree to meet at his.

- Tell a friend or family member that you are meeting someone. As an extra safety measure, you can agree to call your friend/relative or have him call you at a prearranged time to let him know everything is OK. This may seem a bit extreme, but can actually be a good way of getting out of bad dates even if they are not scary or dangerous. I know some people who resort to elaborate ploys to give themselves a realistic-looking way out of potential bad dates. I even know of someone whose method of action is to arrange for a friend to 'run into him' during a date, so he could cut it short if need be. While there's no need to be quite as theatrical, giving yourself a potential way out of a sticky situation can sometimes be a very good thing.

- Always arrange your own transport. Never accept a lift from someone before you have met him in person.

- If your date did not go well and you are going home, politely refuse an offer of a lift and make your own way back.

- Take your mobile phone with you and leave it on at all times. You can put it on silent mode if you have to. While it's considered rude to constantly text or talk on the phone during a date, society has advanced beyond the point where it is expected of you to switch off your mobile completely. You can use your mobile to call for help, in case you ever need to.

- It's perfectly acceptable for a woman to bring a female friend with her to a first date, even if the man she is meeting is coming alone. This is sometimes known as a chaperoned date. For obvious reasons, a friend who is already attached would be a better choice than an attractive single one. Meeting a man in a pub and bringing a friend along is probably one of the most common first date scenarios in the UK. It allows women to go to the pub, have an enjoyable date and drink, without worrying about making bad choices while drunk.

- It's not generally acceptable for a man to bring a friend along to a first date unless you have arranged to go on a double date. In fact, I would go as far as saying that most women would run a mile if two guys turned up to a date instead of just the one.

- You should know your own limit when drinking and be able to make your own decisions about whether alcohol is likely to impair your judgement. Rather than play nanny, I shall leave this matter to your discretion. All I'll say is that if you are aware of a tendency in yourself to make bad decisions when drunk, consider drinking less, unless you have a friend with you.

- If you feel threatened in any way: leave. This is why you chose a public place for your meeting. Don't worry about making a scene; your personal safety must always come first.

- If you are leaving a date because you feel you are in danger, check to see that you are not being followed. Stick to public, well-lit places until you are certain you're safe. If someone is following you, head to the nearest police station or, alternatively, head somewhere public like a shop or a pub and contact the police from there.

■ It's OK to cut a date short if it's not going well. You don't have to feel threatened to do this; not clicking with someone is reason enough. You should be able to end a date simply by saying it's not working for you and be allowed to leave without too much hassle. It's the simplest, most respectful way of ending a bad date. Sometimes, though, you may find yourself in a situation where there is a very good reason for not rejecting someone in an obvious way. In situations where you feel uncomfortable, your first priority is to get yourself out of there. If all else fails, sly tricks will have to do. Go to the toilet, text your friend and ask him to call and give you a reason to leave. Yes, it's obvious and not very nice, but sometimes you just have to do it.

The danger signs

I doubt you need my help in deciding whether or not you are attracted to someone. On the other hand, some character flaws can occasionally slip past our radar, even though they manifest themselves in pretty obvious behavioural traits. Maybe it's because we tend to give people the benefit of the doubt, or maybe we just get stuck in our own bad dating pattern, who knows? Looking back at a bad relationship, we often wonder how we ever missed such obvious signals. In hindsight, everything looks so clear... .

Here are some handy methods you can use to assess your date and see if there's trouble lurking ahead:

■ You can tell a lot about a person by the way he treats the waiters, bar staff or other service staff. A respectful person knows to judge people based on their personality and attitude, not their job or status. A rude and arrogant person will treat them as if their feelings don't matter. Even if this person is nice to you now, beware: this attitude may change if you cross him.

■ Someone who gets too excited too quickly and declares his love on a first date is probably very desperate for love and attention. This could be potential stalker material.

■ Women: beware of anyone who is too physical too quickly, encourages you to get drunk or take drugs (to help you 'relax') or tries to pressure or coerce you into any form of physical contact. Even if the man apologises for his behaviour, the fact that it happened in the first place is a bad sign that should make you very suspicious.

- Past relationships can be the key to understanding someone's character. When talking about this with someone, see if you can find out how many of his exes he is still on good terms with. Someone who is on bad terms with all his exes will probably not be a nice person to deal with if things don't go that well between you.

- If you haven't discussed such matters already while talking online, don't be afraid of steering the conversation in potentially controversial directions on your first date. Realising someone is a bigot on a first date is ten times better than finding out three months later.

Dealing with shyness

Some people communicate better online than they do in person. A date with someone like that can be difficult, especially if you are shy as well. When someone is very shy, he may act in a way that could be confused with being disinterested or aloof, which can make things even worse. Disinterested people usually let their eyes wander around, while shy people tend to keep their gaze low. The two can be easily confused if you don't know what you're looking for. If you are shy, or your date professes to be shy before your date, choose one of the more active first date scenarios such as roller-skating, wine tasting etc. This will give you something to do, as well as something to talk about. If you know that alcohol helps you relax in social situations, there's nothing wrong with going to the pub with your date, as long as you keep the safety rules in mind.

Remember that most shy people open up once they feel comfortable, so even if a date starts off a bit awkwardly, things may pick up later or on the next date. This is especially true if your online conversations have been going well.

Who pays for the first date?

Obviously, the safest option is to split the bill, as this leaves no room for misunderstandings. I know most men who offer to pay for dinner do it for the right reasons, but there are still a few weirdos out there who expect something in return. Going Dutch makes this a non-issue for everyone involved. If you are splitting the bill, don't be petty about it. Being tight with money is not an attractive quality and it's better to lose out on a few pounds than to make yourself instantly unappealing to your date.

If one person is to pay, then it will always be the man; it seems that some things never change. I don't believe women should *expect* the man to pay, but if he's offering, there isn't necessarily anything wrong with accepting. It's up to you to judge the situation and decide whether this is an honest gentlemanly gesture or something more sinister. Usually, it's the former rather than the latter, but you never know. It almost goes without saying that any man who asks a woman to pay for dinner is likely to end up dateless very fast.

Should I bring her flowers?

Never bring a bouquet of flowers to a first date. Things have moved on from times when this was acceptable and welcome behaviour. The majority of women would find such a gesture exaggerated and possibly even freaky. This is because most men nowadays only bring flowers when they have done something wrong or on occasions such as anniversaries and birthdays. Bringing flowers, even a rose, could be taken as a signal that you have already decided that a romantic relationship is on the cards. This could make the woman feel that you are trying to pressure her into making a decision she is not yet ready to make. Save these gestures for further down the line when you both know how you feel about each other.

Should I sleep with him on the first date?

Just the fact that I get asked this question is enough to show the imbalance there is in our society. No man ever gets criticised for sleeping with someone on a first date, whereas women often have to consider their reputation. Regardless of how you may feel about that, this is still an issue that needs to be considered.

Never sleep with someone on a first date if you are doing it because:

- **You are too drunk to stop and think whether or not you really want to**. Were you not sure about whether or not you wanted to sleep with this person before? Has it been looking more and more like a viable option the more you had to drink? If so, this is probably not a good idea.

- **You feel it is expected of you.** Whatever someone says or does, your body is your own and you don't owe anyone anything. Any decent man would be horrified to think a woman went to bed with him for any reason other than her wanting to do so. Men who don't feel this way are too sleazy and disgusting for their feelings to be taken into account at all. Like traditional dating, online dating has no rules that state when you should sleep with anyone and under what circumstances. The decision is entirely up to you.

■ **You want to 'seal the deal' on the date**. If a man is interested in more than just a one-night stand with you, he will wait until you are ready to sleep with him. Don't be tempted into sleeping with anyone before you feel that it's the right time for you to do it.

■ **Any other reason that is not a result of an informed decision on your behalf.** Not all men are the same and not all women are the same. Sadly, there are plenty of men out there who lose respect for women who sleep with them 'too soon'. As strange and disgusting as this prejudice may seem, it's very real. Sadly, this attitude is not exclusive to religious people with traditional family values etc. Men who feel this way can pop up on the most liberal and seemingly open-minded scenes. However, there are some men out there for whom this is a non-issue. At the end of the day, a woman's body is her own and you should be able to do as you please with yours. If your aim is to live your life in your own way and find a man who is free of such social constraints then that's great and I wish you good luck. However, be prepared to deal with the consequences associated with following your own path if you choose to go against society's conventions. Strong women often find themselves alone.

Beyond the first date

If your first date is successful, the online part of your dating experience can be put to rest. There is no need to keep communicating via the site unless it is particularly convenient for you both to do so. As this is a book about online dating, I won't try and tell you how to run your offline love life but some of the same rules that apply online are bound to apply in the real world as well:

■ Be yourself (but show your best side to begin with)

■ Don't be too aloof: if you are interested, it's OK to say that you are

■ Don't be too pushy: clearly stating your interest is enough. Let things progress slowly and gently if need be, without putting any pressure on the other person to constantly see you or speak to you

■ Feel free to keep seeing other people for a while if you are uncertain, but try to be honest about it rather than pretend to be exclusive

In all cases, enjoy your dating experience, especially if you've been out of the game for a while.

Chapter 11

When things go wrong

In this chapter you will find out about:

■ Knowing where the problem lies

■ Common problems and their solutions

Hopefully, by this point in this book, you will have learned enough about online dating to be able to get some good results. However, sometimes things don't go as planned. This chapter is here to help you address common problems and get yourself out of a rut, should you happen to find yourself in one.

Is it the site or is it me?

Generally, there are two reasons why things could go wrong with your online dating experience:

1. You are doing something to hinder your own chances

2. You are on a dating site that's just not right for you

The fact is, not all dating sites will be right for you. Even sites that seemingly cater to the same niche may differ from each other greatly in the sort of clientele they attract. If you establish that the site you are on is wrong for you: leave. There is no point wasting more of your time and money on there. What you want to avoid, though, is a situation where the problem lies elsewhere — something you have written in your profile, perhaps, or a picture that sends the wrong message — and is carried with you to every website you try.

In most cases, it's possible to know whether a site is potentially right for you just by running a search and reading people's profiles. However, sometimes things only become apparent later on, when you realise the people on there are not what they first seemed. If you can't find a single person on the site you would like to contact, then the problem is most likely the site and not you. Even on sites that offer matching based on a personality test, you can usually tweak the results offered by the matching system by retaking the test or sections of it. If the site continues to give you bad matches: move on.

Of course, if you've tried 15 different sites and can't find anyone you want to talk to, then either you are not yet ready to date again or online dating is not for you.

Taking a look at yourself

Imagine how much easier life would be if we could take a step back from ourselves when on a date, examine our behaviour from the outside and note all the things we do that may send the wrong signal to the other person. With online dating we can do this to an extent, as we can read what we have written critically and see how it could be read by others.

In my experience, the majority of problems can be solved by taking a good look at the profile, the picture and the messages sent to others. When troubleshooting your online dating experience, it helps to be methodical. Start by assuming that your problem lies in one of these aforementioned areas and check them one by one until you are satisfied that they are all as good as they should be. Once you've established that, you can look at other reasons, like the site being wrong for you.

Common problems and possible reasons behind them

'No one replies to any of my messages'

It can be quite distressing when you put yourself out there and get nothing back. The following case studies will help give you insight into possible reasons why this might happen.

Case study 1

The problem: A man who finds Asian women very attractive signed up to an Asian dating site, although not Asian himself. He contacted many women but got no responses.

The solution: The women on that particular site had joined it because they were interested in meeting Asian men from their own communities. This is hardly surprising, when you consider the fact that those women had chosen an Asian dating site rather than a general membership site.

If you choose a niche or orientation site, make sure it's one where you fit in. While some sites accommodate people who don't fit the bill themselves, others don't. You would be wasting your time and money if you placed yourself on the wrong site. The man in the example above could have had the world's best-written profile and a very attractive picture and it wouldn't have made any difference: the women on that site would still not be interested.

It's not only niche and orientation sites that have standards that need to be adhered to. Some sites simply attract people with certain political views, world outlooks, education level, professions, etc. If your search keeps bringing up the wrong people, go somewhere else.

Case study 2

The problem: A man once wrote to our customer service team and asked for his money back. He said that he had been on the site for several months, sent many messages and didn't get a single reply. After some investigating, it turned out the man had not yet uploaded a photo, the description in his profile said 'I am a guy looking for girls' and every single message he'd sent had been either overtly rude or short and generic. It was no wonder he'd never received a reply.

The solution: A good profile, a photo, well-written messages and a respectful attitude are essential when trying to get people to respond to you. Don't skimp on such details as they are all important. If you are certain that everything you have written is OK, contact the customer service team and ask for their advice. They will be able to check whether your messages have been delivered and also tell you if there are any problems with your profile you are not aware of.

'I seem to only attract freaks/men who want sex/stalkers/abusive guys/gold-diggers/time wasters'

Case study 1

The problem: A woman had written to complain that she was getting a lot of unwelcome attention from men on the site. She said all of the men who had contacted her had asked her for 'web chats' straight away and seemed to only be interested in sex. I suspected that this may be the usual case of an over-revealing photo on her profile, but her photo was pretty standard although she was quite an attractive woman. Her profile, on the other hand, was very sparse.

The solution: If you rely on your looks alone to attract people, you will attract people who are only interested in your looks. Always make sure to write about yourself so that your profile has an appeal beyond the obvious. While this may not dissuade the sex-seekers from contacting you, it would help you attract the more interesting people.

Case study 2

The problem: A woman consistently met men through dating sites who seemed OK at the beginning but then turned out to be emotionally unavailable with severe commitment problems. She checked her profile to see if there was anything there that could attract them but couldn't find anything out of the ordinary.

The solution: Unfortunately, someone who has a bad dating pattern is likely to find it repeating itself both on and off the Internet. If you have been with several people who exhibited more or less the same problems (i.e.being abusive, unavailable, dishonest etc.) then there may be a reason why you are attracted to them in the first place. I am not suggesting that you should necessarily forgive those who have hurt you because it was you who were attracted to them, but it may be time to sit down and have a think about why it is that you seek out people who treat you this way. There could be many reasons for this and they are obviously going to be different from person to person. How you address these issues is up to you. You may want to seek counselling, speak to friends, read self-help books or simply let yourself heal at your own pace before dating again.

'I get a response to my first message, but then people stop talking to me after we continue messaging/meet up in person'

Case study 1

The problem: A woman started dating on a certain site and soon got a response from a man she was interested in. She had been on her own for a while after a bad break-up and so was excited to find someone she liked so much so quickly. She would send the man several messages a day while she was at work or at home, telling him about her day and asking him about his. She became concerned when he didn't reply as quickly as she'd have liked and became worried that he might not like her as much as she liked him. She suspected he may be talking to other women as well and it bothered her. When they had their first date, everything seemed to go well. She started calling the man several times a day to suggest they meet up again, go out to the same places, etc. Whenever he refused, she became suspicious and demanded to know whether he was seeing someone else. Unfortunately, the man seemed to not take this very well and told her it was over a week later.

The solution: Both men and women can get ahead of themselves after the first date or even while still talking online. While I am not a fan of the school of thought that states you should treat people badly to make them want you, a certain sense of decorum is still called for here. The woman in this example was acting out of desperation and fear of being alone. Neither of those are attractive qualities in a person. While women are often the ones being blamed for this type of behaviour, some men are just as guilty of being overbearing and desperate. Such behaviour would only have a negative effect on a relationship. If someone is not interested, no amount of contact on your behalf will make him want you. On the other hand, even someone who is interested could be put off by not being given enough space. If you are interested in someone, make it clear but be respectful and pace yourself. Keeping your options open and seeing other people can also help, as it would take the pressure off making a particular relationship succeed until you are sure you are really interested.

Chapter 12

Other ways of meeting people online

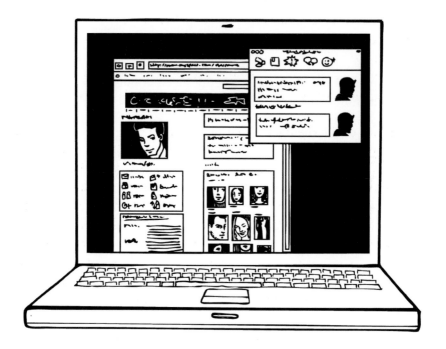

In this chapter you will find out about:

■ Chats and online personals

■ Social networking sites and communities

■ Blogs and forums

■ Online games

Alternatives to online dating sties

Up until now, I've concentrated on the obvious method of online dating, i.e. the kind that involves using dedicated dating sites. Obviously, people have been using the Internet for dating long before the first dating site appeared. Even today, a lot of online dating activity happens away from dating sites. This chapter will give you an overview of the alternatives on offer. Some of these alternatives are remnants from times before the advent of dating sites and are now virtually obsolete. Others can complement your dating experience or even provide a viable alternative. While I do believe that dating sites are the safest, most effective online dating method, I think these other methods deserve a mention too, if you want to get the complete picture.

The majority of the mediums listed in this chapter were not designed to facilitate dating but rather human interaction in general. There is no guarantee that the people you meet under these circumstances will be single and interested in dating of any kind. Because of this, these methods are not suitable for everyone. If you are looking for quick results, stick with standard dating sites. The alternative methods listed here are more suitable if you want to take your time, make new friends, find people to share your interests and hobbies and expand your social life at a slower pace. There is no guarantee you would meet the love of your life like this, but then again there is no guarantee you'd meet him on a proper dating site either.

I know many happy couples who met each other through message boards, online communities and even mailing lists. Along the way, they made many good friends, went on regular social outings and generally had fun. If you've tried some dating sites and didn't enjoy the experience, maybe this is where you should be looking next.

This chapter is by no means a comprehensive guide to any of the mediums listed. My intention is rather to show you what's out there – the good and the bad – so that you can go off and explore anything you find interesting.

Online personals

Examples: Gumtree.com, craigslist.org

The first of the online dating dinosaurs, online personals used to be very popular before dating sites were invented. They are still commonly used today.

What they are there for

Online personals usually exist as part of larger noticeboard sites where people can post ads about other stuff as well. Sometimes the ads appear on sites associated with newspapers or magazines and are effectively the electronic version of the printed lonely-heart personals. These ads are supposedly there to help people find love, but in reality provide a different service altogether.

How they work

Posting or answering an online personal ad is pretty straightforward. The most you would generally need to provide when posting an ad is a name and an email address. The ads are generally free to answer and often free to post. The only exceptions are ad sections on community sites that charge for membership or paid ad sites like Loot.com.

The experience

Because they are free and anonymous, online personals attract exactly the type of sleazy perverts standard dating sites work so hard to filter out. This is especially true on the free and easily accessible sites where anyone can post an ad without being vetted. Forget about finding love here; most people only want one-night stands and casual sex. Craig's list, for example, is notorious for being the Internet's version of a sleazy pick-up joint.

If you do decide to meet someone through a personal ad, be extremely careful: many of the horror stories about online dating happened as a result of answering online personal ads, rather than using a dating site. Refer to the safety tips in Chapters 8 and 9 and make sure you follow them to the letter.

Etiquette issues

While a certain element of decorum is generally expected of people who post personal ads, some people choose to ignore this. Many of the ads are pretty graphic or sexual in nature and some are outright strange. On the other hand, as this is a dedicated service for people who want to meet up for a date (or sex), you would not be ruffling anyone's feathers by asking for a date (or sex).

Conclusion

Most of the bad things you may have heard about online dating can be experienced by trying online personals. The only people who still use them are hardcore nerds, perverts and people who are yet to discover dating sites. Avoid at all cost, unless you really are looking for a quick, anonymous shag.

Chats/chat rooms

Before dating sites came along, chats were the best way to meet people online. They are the closest thing you can have to a real conversation online, with many platforms now offering video and voice chat. Nowadays, their popularity as a place to meet new people is declining.

What they are there for

Chat networks and chat rooms exist everywhere on the Internet. There are chat networks that are independent of the Web such as MSN messenger, AOL Instant Messenger, ICQ, IRC, etc. and there are even chat systems that exist as part of peer-to-peer networks like *Soulseek*. Some networks offer chat rooms dedicated to dating and romance while others are more generic in nature. Many websites offer chat rooms too, especially community sites, which are discussed later on in this chapter.

How they work

Chat networks usually require you to download and install a program called a 'client' that you will then use to connect to the network. You will also need to set up an account on the network. Once all that's done, you will be able to search for people or join 'rooms' or 'channels' where you can speak to others. Chat rooms that exist as part of a website will usually appear in your web browser. You may be required to download a plug-in to make the chat application work.

The experience

Chat networks are often lawless places. Similar to online personals, these are now a haven for scammers, spammers, criminals and perverts. Chats are often frequented by people interested in having cybersex. If you use a feminine nickname for your chat session you will probably be inundated with requests. It's a well-known fact that many of the 'women' who hang out in chat rooms are actually men in disguise, but that doesn't seem to stop people from trying it on. As a result, many chat rooms have now become very cliquey, suspecting newcomers of being perverts until proven otherwise.

Websites that offer chat rooms vary greatly in atmosphere, moderating standards and clientele. Those belonging to large, well-established companies are likely to be moderated, sometimes to the point of being unsuitable for the purposes of online dating. On sites that cater for minors as well as adults you may not be allowed to share any personal details at all. Other sites may offer a more lenient moderation policy, or none at all.

Etiquette

Not all chat rooms are suitable for the purposes of dating. If a chat room is dedicated to a different topic altogether, such as flower arranging or country music, you may find that the majority of people who hang out there are interested in discussing the actual topic at hand. Some of the people may even be attached already, or even married. It's considered bad form to join a non-dating-related chat room for the sole purpose of finding a date. You must be able (and willing) to discuss the main topic of the chat room if you are to fit in.

Conclusion

The time for meeting random people through online chat networks has sadly past. This is a method best suited for keeping in touch with people you've met by other means. As a dating method in its own right, it's generally a total waste of time. It may be possible to meet someone nice through a chat network, but such occasions are hardly common.

Chat rooms on websites are often OK, as long as you adhere to the safety and etiquette rules listed earlier in this book.

Social networking sites

Examples: Myspace.com, Friendster.com, Tribe.net

Even though we often compare dating sites to bars and clubs, they are really more like singles' nights. Social networking sites are more like the parties you would go to in order to socialise with friends, relatives, colleagues, etc. You may well meet other singles there, but that is not an essential part of the experience.

Social networking sites are often fairly similar in appearance to dating sites; many of them do actually offer some dating features, although often of the basic variety. These sites are based on the concept of expanding your social life outwardly through your friends. Many were inspired by the concept of 'six degrees of separation', that claims all the people in the world are connected to each other by a string of acquaintances numbering no more than five. Whether or not that is true, spending any time on a social networking site is likely to show you just how small our world is.

Social networking sites were hailed as the natural successors to dating sites and an alternative for people who wanted to avoid the stigma. Now that the online dating stigma is virtually a non-issue, it turns out that social networking sites exist in a niche of their own. Many members of such sites prefer to use them in order to stay in touch with existing groups of friends, rather than make new romantic connections.

In terms of online dating, social networking sites can be useful for:

- Meeting people on the outskirts of your social scene
- Meeting people based on mutual interests
- Searching or browsing for singles based on simple age/sex/location criteria

How it works

You set up a profile in a similar way you would on a dating site and upload photos, etc. You can then start searching for friends and adding them to your list. These can be actual friends of yours, new people you want to get to know or your favourite band, celebrity or even politicians (Conservative leader, David Cameron, is known to have a Myspace account). Once connected to these 'friends' you can browse their friends and their friends' friends, message people, post bulletins, comments or photos and so on.

The experience

Social networking sites are generally free to use and are supported by advertising. They are usually moderated reactively, rather than proactively, meaning that members and their photos are not vetted at the time of joining. It's up to you to complain about anything or anyone you find offensive and make the moderators take a look.

Most social networking sites have an international membership, but when you search for singles, you can limit your searches to people in your local area.

Profiles on social networking sites are very similar to personal homepages and many people use them as a free, easy alternative to writing a personal website. Such profiles are generally more customisable than those on dating sites: you can change the background and text colour, add pretty pictures, music, etc. Because of the nature of these sites, it's perfectly OK to upload pictures where your face isn't showing. In fact, you can upload pictures that are not of you at all.

Unlike dating sites, where the preferred mode of communication is one-on-one, social networking sites are usually very public. Friends are openly displayed on each user's profiles and people often choose to communicate by leaving public comments on each other's pages. As a result, the whole thing looks a bit like a giant popularity contest, where people are encouraged to add more and more friends, collect public comments and befriend the many bands, artists and celebrities who are represented on the sites.

To enhance their experience, members can form discussion groups and enjoy their own message boards. On the big sites there are thousands of groups covering just about every topic under the sun.

Etiquette

Sites such as Myspace.com have now become a bit of a social hub for their members, who use them to create a virtual space for keeping in touch with their friends. As a result, things can get quite cliquey at times, with people not being open to communicating with strangers. Unlike on dating sites, you cannot immediately assume that the people on a social networking site all want the same thing as you do. Many of the people who frequent the sites are already attached. Others may only be interested in meeting people they are directly connected to.

On most sites, users can specify what they are looking for (friendship, networking, dating, etc.). If you are running a search for people to talk to, make sure you include only people whose profile states they are interested in dating. Once you've done that, you can continue as if you were on a standard dating site.

It is considered bad form to send a friend request to a stranger without introducing yourself first. Usually people will refuse the friendship request under such circumstances. The only exceptions are when trying to 'friend' bands and celebrities who are only really there for the publicity anyway.

When joining a discussion group, read a few posts first to see what sort of behaviour people expect. Some groups can be quite cliquey and it's easy to make a faux pas when you don't know the rules. In most cases, if you are polite and friendly you will quickly make friends.

Conclusion

Many people have met and fallen in love after meeting on social networking sites. People use them for dating all the time. In general, they are mostly suited for the 18-45 age bracket, although the number of older members is constantly growing. As another free, unmoderated medium, social networking sites tend to draw their fair share of scammers and other unwelcome guests, but you can easily block any troublesome users.

Forums, groups and message boards

Forums and message boards exist practically everywhere on the Internet. Just about every website out there will offer some sort of message board for people to interact on. Forums vary in prominence and popularity, but are highly popular as a method of interaction.

What they are there for

Some forums exist purely for social interaction, while others are there to offer support, share information or discuss various topics related to the theme of the website they're on. There are thousands of forums out there, for any topic you can think of, both local and international.

In terms of dating, forums and message boards can be useful for:

■ Meeting people who share your interests

■ Finding activity partners

■ Becoming part of a community

How it works

Forums and message boards are everywhere. Some exist as part of larger websites, while others are there just for the sake of being there. When checking out forums, you can usually read the messages (posts) without signing up, but most forums will require you to register in order to post anything yourself. Generally forums are free to use unless they are a part of a paid membership site.

Forum interaction is usually done on the website itself, although discussion groups such as the ones on Yahoo! Groups, Google Groups etc. can also be emailed to you in the form of a mailing list.

Communication on forums and message boards is usually public in nature: everyone will see the messages you post. When you are registered, some forums allow you to send private messages too.

When using forums for dating and socialising purposes, try looking for domestic or even local forums, so that you can easily attend any meet-ups.

The experience

Not all forums are suitable for online dating. Some, like most of the BBC forums, for example, don't allow people to share personal information at all. While you can use those forums to talk to people who share your interests, you would not be able to take things offsite unless you manage to outsmart the moderators.

Other forums are not necessarily moderated at all and, in most cases, users are not vetted before joining. If you are going to meet anyone off a forum, make sure you follow the safety rules.

Forums are great if you have a particular hobby or interest that you want to explore while meeting like-minded people. If you are the sort of person who prefers long introductions and friendship before romance then forums could be perfect for you. This type of social interaction could provide you with an instant social group. Obviously, if you hang out on a photographers' forum, chances are that many people on there would be interested in speaking about photography and not much else. There is no guarantee that any of them would be interested in dating. However, many such forums organise group outings and trips, which are a great way of pursuing your hobby while making new friends. If you do meet someone via a forum (and many people do), you will already know you have at least one thing in common.

Forums are basically little social groups or communities. If you spend a bit of time following posts in a forum, you will soon know who the main players are and what sort of behaviour is expected of members. Some groups even have their own list of rules posted somewhere and it's worth reading those first before posting. This may seem a bit overly dramatic and involved (and sometimes it is) but in most cases is just a way of making sure the group or forum functions in an efficient manner. Like any other social groups, you will find some places are more welcoming than others. If you come across some cliquey, unfriendly people move on: there are plenty of other places to try.

Etiquette

Unless you are on a forum, message board or group that exists especially for the purposes of dating, don't use it as if it were a dating site: people will react badly. Going onto a forum, introducing yourself and immediately inquiring about singles would be about as welcome as joining a serious dating site and asking for sex.

Always ask yourself: 'if I weren't looking for a date, or knew I couldn't find one here, would I still want to speak to people on this forum?' If the answer is no, then the forum is not for you.

Forums have topics of discussion and people tend to dislike off-topic posts. Some forums have several sections with one dedicated to general socialising. This is where you should head first to do your meeting and greeting.

People appreciate it when you take time to read their post and write relevant replies. This is not entirely unlike commenting on things in someone's profile when contacting him for the first time. I've seen cases where people were keen to 'get their faces known' on a forum and chose to reply to a large number of posts by saying things like 'I agree!' and 'that's so true'. Unfortunately, all that did was clutter the forum with lots of nonsensical posts that ended up annoying everyone. A few relevant posts that add something to the forum are going to make a much better impression than trying to reply to everyone all the time.

Some people tend to take their online hang-outs rather seriously at times. In fact, sometimes they take them far too seriously. Some of the people who hang out on online forums and discussion groups don't have much of a social life away from the Internet. As a rule, the more active someone is online, the less likely he is to have an active life offline. Don't be tempted to try and point this out to people. It never works. Experience shows that people usually react badly when asked to 'lighten up' or 'keep things in proportion'.

Conclusion

Forums are generally good for making friends. You won't necessarily meet any attractive singles, or even unattractive ones, but you never know. If you are in need of a new social group, activity partners or emotional support then forums and groups can definitely help.

Online gaming

These have been around for years and are more popular than ever. As technology advances, these games get more and more involved. Even game consoles can now be connected to the Internet.

What they are there for

The Internet is full of multi-user games, from backgammon to sword-and-sorcery role-playing games of various descriptions. People join them predominantly for the sake of playing the game in question, although some games have whole online communities based around them.

How they work

Games can be easily found by searching; there are millions of them. Make sure you search for 'multi-user games', as you want to find games where you can play with other people.

Many games are free, although some operate as paid membership sites. In all cases, you will need to register. Most gaming sites will offer some sort of messaging or chat feature, either public or private, which people use in order to communicate with each other while playing.

Have a look around first to see what moderation policy is employed by the site. As gaming sites often have an appeal to kids, some sites may not allow the sharing of personal details.

The experience

Unless you are a gamer yourself, you may find these sites rather dull. Most gamers get very absorbed when playing their online games and not all will have the time or inclination to stop and chat.

Members of gaming sites that are more community-based will often arrange meet-ups, go to the pub together and generally hang out and chat when not playing the game. Find one of those and you may end up with a whole load of new friends.

Most gaming communities are international and some may not have a large UK membership. It's often impossible to know who the members are, where they are from or even if they are male or female. Age is also an issue, as many of those sites cater to kids.

Etiquette

People generally join gaming communities in order to play the game. They react badly to people who have no interest in the game and only join in order to meet other people.

Because of the age issue, it's common to ask people how old they are. If you are chatting to someone online, ask sooner rather than later to avoid any awkward situations.

Conclusion

These can help pass the time and make friends, but are not very reliable as a dating method. If you are a die-hard gamer looking to date someone similar, these communities could be a good place to start but, as usual, there are no guarantees.

Blogs and online communities

Examples: blogger.com, livejournal.com, flickr.com

Hailed as the future of the Internet, blogs (or web logs) are an extremely popular personal-publishing and social interaction tool.

What they are there for

Blogs are basically public online diaries. Bloggers use these to talk about their daily lives, rant about things that annoy them, tell about interesting websites they've seen and so on. Blogging communities allow bloggers to link up with each other, comment on each other's blogs and get notified when their favourite blogs are being updated. Some blogs are meant as a way for people to let their friends and family know what's going on in their lives. Others are more public and can be about less personal topics. Many companies now operate their own blogs to keep in touch with their customers and blogging is now considered a good way of raising one's professional profile. Apart from blogging communities, there are other types of online communities dedicated to sharing photos, music, etc. that operate in a similar fashion.

How they work

Blogs and online communities are not entirely dissimilar to social networking sites. In fact, many social networking sites now offer a blogging feature. Unlike social networking sites you are not likely to be able to run an age/sex/location search for people to talk to, but can usually search for other blogs based on location or topic.

You can create a blog by signing up to one of the free (or paid) blogging websites. You can usually set up a sort of basic profile with a description, list of interests and some photos. You can browse other people's blogs, add those people as friends, make comments, send messages etc. Once set up, you can start writing your own blog and update it as often as you like.

The experience

Blogs and other similar communities were not designed for the purposes of dating, but they do encourage communication between people all over the world. On most online communities, you can easily link up with others and create a network. On some sites (such as Livejournal.com) people tend to stick together in private cliques, although you can specify a list of interests and meet people who share those interests with you. On photo-sharing communities such as Flickr.com you can browse people's photos and add people to your contact list. You can communicate by sending private messages or leaving comments on each other's profiles.

Etiquette

There are some blogs about dating out there and certainly plenty of blogs by singles who want to find love. Blogging in general, though, although public by nature, is not necessarily geared towards online dating. Women bloggers are particularly sensitive to unsolicited advances and may get quite annoyed if contacted in what they perceive as a disrespectful manner.

When browsing blogging sites, you can make yourself known by responding to other people's blog posts, commenting on photos etc. As with forum posts, it's best not to do it in a way that would appear as if you are just doing it for the sake of getting noticed.

When writing your own blog, you can get a wider readership by writing about things that go beyond your day-to-day routines. Write about issues you feel strongly about, share tips about things you are good at or write about your experiences of learning new skills. You could even write about your attempts at finding love. After all, that's a subject anyone can relate to.

In the anarchic world of the Internet, it's relatively easy to become a minor celebrity if you have something new or useful to say. Who knows who you might meet if you put some thought into your writing?

Conclusion

Although these were not at all designed for dating, they are a great way of putting yourself out there and meeting new people. Blogs can also provide a good place for you to work through any personal issues of the type that don't belong on a dating site (past break-ups, etc.).

Appendixes

Appendix 1

Useful links

Dating sites

Dating for Parents:	http://www.datingforparents.com
DatingDirect:	http://www.datingdirect.com
Gorgeous Dating:	http://www.gorgeousdating.com
Guardian Soulmates:	http://www.guardiansoulmates.com
Jdate:	http://www.jdate.com
Loopylove:	http://www.loopylove.com
Match:	http://uk.match.com/
My Single Friend:	http://www.mysinglefriend.com
Ok Cupid:	http://www.okcupid.com
Parship:	http://www.parship.co.uk

Social networking sites

Friendster:	http://www.friendster.com
Myspace:	http://www.myspace.com

Safety-related sites

Dating scam advice:

http://www.oft.gov.uk/Consumer/Scams/Online+dating+scams.htm

Supportline stalking advice:

http://www.supportline.org.uk/problems/stalking.php

Bullyonline cyberstalking and cyberbullying advice:

http://www.bullyonline.org/related/stalking.htm

The Network for Surviving Stalking:

http://www.nss.org.uk

Appendix 2

Common online abbreviations and codes

Abbreviations

AFAIK	As far as I know
ASAP	As soon as possible
BBL	Be back later
BBS	Be back soon
Blog	Web log
BRB	Be right back
BTW	By the way
F2F	Face to face
FOAF	Friend of a friend
FWIW	For what it's worth
FYI	For your information
GSOH	Great sense of humour
GTG (or **G2G**)	Got to go
IM	Instant Messaging
IMHO	In my honest opinion
IMO	In my opinion
IRL	In real life (offline, away from the Internet)
IYKWIM	If you know what I mean
JK or **J/K**	Just kidding
K	OK
LOL	Laugh out loud

MYOB	Mind your own business
NP	No problem
OIC	Oh, I see
OMG	Oh my god
OTOH	On the other hand
PM	Private message
RL	Real life
ROFLMAO	Rolling on floor laughing my arse off
ROFL	Rolling on floor laughing
ROTFL	Rolling on the floor laughing
SPAM	Stupid pointless annoying message (junk email)
Thnx/Tnx/Tx	Thanks
TTFN	Ta ta for now
TTYL	Talk to you later
U	You
WB	Welcome back
WYSIWYG	What you see is what you get

Codes

Adult fun	One-night stand, sex, casual relationship
Camera fun/ Adult camera chat/ Webcam chat	Cybersex or live-camera sex chat
Discreet no strings fun	A casual relationship with a married/ attached person
No strings fun	A casual relationship/casual sex

Index

Get a free week on Loopylove.com!★

LoopyLove.com has an unpretentious approach to dating that isn't reserved for beautiful people. Our members are real and everyone is welcome. With over a million members and a thousand more joining every day, it's no wonder we're one of the UK's favourite dating sites.

To make use of a **free week's full membership**, open a free account by logging on to http://www.loopylove.com and signing up with your details.

Then fill out your details below and send this coupon to:

Loopylove Dating Guide Promotion
Allegran Limited
1st Floor East
3-5 Bleeding Heart Yard
LONDON
EC1N 8SJ

★ One offer per person. Offer valid until 30th May 2008

Please give me a free week's full membership on Loopylove.com!

Name:_____

Email address:_____

Postal address:_____

_____